CW01084160

INVITATION TO JOIN THE GOVERNMENT OF BRITAIN

THE CONSERVATIVE MANIFESTO 2010

INVITATION TO JOIN THE GOVERNMENT OF BRITAIN

A country is at its best when the bonds between people are strong and when the sense of national purpose is clear. Today the challenges facing Britain are immense. Our economy is overwhelmed by debt, our social fabric is frayed and our political system has betrayed the people. But these problems can be overcome if we pull together and work together. If we remember that we are all in this together.

Some politicians say: 'give us your vote and we will sort out all your problems'. We say: real change comes not from government alone. Real change comes when the people are inspired and mobilised, when millions of us are fired up to play a part in the nation's future.

Yes this is ambitious. Yes it is optimistic. But in the end all the Acts of Parliament, all the new measures, all the new policy initiatives, are just politicians' words without you and your involvement.

How will we deal with the debt crisis unless we understand that we are all in this together? How will we raise responsible children unless every adult plays their part? How will we revitalise communities unless people stop asking 'who will fix this?' and start asking 'what can I do?' Britain will change for the better when we all elect to take part, to take responsibility – if we all come together. Collective strength will overpower our problems.

Only together can we can get rid of this government and, eventually, its debt. Only together can we get the economy moving. Only together can we protect the NHS. Improve our schools. Mend our broken society. Together we can even make politics and politicians work better. And if we can do that, we can do anything. Yes, together we can do anything.

So my invitation today is this: join us, to form a new kind of government for Britain.

CONTENTS

CONTENTS

This manifesto is available in braille, easyread, large print and audio.
Please call 020 7222 9000 to request a copy, or visit our website
www.conservatives.com.

Britain needs change: few can doubt that. Our national finances are mired in massive debt. Millions are living the misery of unemployment. Communities are shattered by crime and abuse. People in the public services are trapped in a web of rules and regulations. People have lost faith that politics can fix our problems, or that politicians can lead us into a better future. There is a feeling of helplessness. Once again, there is a mood afoot that the decline of Britain is inevitable.

But there is no law that says we must accept decline. We have the energy, the ideas and the ambition to get Britain back on track. And that includes everyone in Britain, wherever they live and whatever their circumstances. If we join together, if we act decisively, and move forward with optimism, we can start to fix the economic, social and political problems that threaten the nation. We can bring about the change Britain needs.

What is that change? Some promise solutions from on high – but real change comes from collective endeavour. So we offer a new approach: a change not just from one set of politicians to another; from one set of policies to another. It is a change from one political philosophy to another. From the idea that the role of the state is to direct society and micro-manage public services, to the idea that the role of the state is to strengthen society and make public services serve the people who use them. In a simple phrase, the change we offer is from big government to Big Society.

This manifesto is the most important stage so far on a journey that began four and a half years ago, when the Conservative Party itself voted for change by electing David Cameron as its leader. Since then, the Party has remoulded itself for the modern era, applying its deepest values and beliefs to the urgent problems of the hour. Even as it has done so, the problems confronting Britain have escalated, and escalated fast. So our ideas are ambitious and radical as well as modern. They match the scale of Britain's problems, and are in tune with a world that is changing before our eyes. But our core values have not altered and our core beliefs remain consistent.

We believe in responsibility: government responsibility with public finances, personal responsibility for our actions, and social responsibility towards each other. We believe in enterprise and aspiration. We believe there is such a thing as society, it's just not the same thing as the state. Our fundamental tenet is that power should be devolved from politicians to people, from the central to the local. Personal ambition should be set as high as is humanly possible, with no barriers put in its way by the state. Perhaps most importantly, we believe that we are all in this together.

Everything you will find in this manifesto is built on these beliefs. They are the building blocks of the change we want to see in every home, every street, every community, every business.

Our belief in responsibility with public finances is the starting point of our **plan for economic recovery and growth**. We want your consent for a programme of public spending control that will deal with Labour's debt crisis and stop the Labour jobs tax that would kill our economic recovery. The programme set out in this manifesto is fully costed and fully funded. Some of our proposals – such as on school discipline – cost nothing, but require energy and leadership. Others – like stopping Labour's jobs tax – will require money, and we will make savings in other areas to pay for them. The debt crisis is the terrible legacy that Gordon Brown is bequeathing to our country. But fiscal responsibility needs a social conscience or it is not responsible at all: so we will not allow the poorest people in Britain to pay an unfair price for the mistakes of some of the richest.

Nor will we allow irresponsibility in the private sector to continue unchecked. We will bring law and order to our financial markets as a necessary step to restoring confidence. But the real prize for Britain is to create a new economic model, one founded on investment and savings not borrowing and debt. This economic vision reflects our belief in enterprise and aspiration. It is a vision of a truly modern economy: one that is greener and more local. An economy where Britain leads in science, technology and innovation. But it is founded on a determination that wealth and opportunity must be more fairly distributed. We want to see an economy where not just our standard of living, but everyone's quality of life, rises steadily and sustainably.

But a nation is only really successful if it is built on a **strong society**. We will never deal with our debts and build a new economy unless we solve the social problems that cost so much and hold so many people back. Labour's big government approach is making our social problems worse, not better – inequality and poverty on the rise; social mobility stalled; family breakdown a fact of life for too many children. So we need fundamental change: from big government that presumes to know best, to the Big Society that trusts in the people for ideas and innovation.

We will move from state action to social action, encouraging social responsibility in all its forms and across all the country – whether curbing incivility on our streets or supporting social enterprises with the power to transform neighbourhoods. Mending Britain's broken society will be a central aim of the next Conservative government.

That is why in this manifesto we set ourselves an ambitious goal: to make Britain the most family-friendly country in Europe. That is why we back the NHS. That is why we will reform schools to raise standards and restore discipline. It is why we will get people off benefits and into work; reform policing, sentencing and prisons. And why we are committed to a greener future.

But we will not succeed in building the Big Society, or in building a new economic model, unless we stop government trying to direct everything from the centre. We will get nowhere with yet more top-down state control. So, after thirteen years of Labour, we need **radical political reform**. We need to change the whole way this country is run. As Conservatives, we trust people. We believe that if people are given more responsibility, they will behave more responsibly. We believe that if you decentralise power, you get better results and better value for money. So the plans set out in this manifesto represent an unprecedented redistribution of power and control from the central to the local, from politicians and the bureaucracy to individuals, families and neighbourhoods.

We will give people much more say over the things that affect their daily lives. We will make government, politics and public services much more open and transparent. And we will give the people who work in our public services much greater responsibility. But in return, they will have to answer to the people. All these measures will help restore trust in our broken political system.

We know that this is an ambitious vision. A profoundly optimistic vision. It is also an authentically Conservative vision: sound money, backing enterprise, trusting people. The journey we embarked on four and a half years ago was all about applying this Conservative approach to the progressive challenges of our age: making opportunity more equal; fighting poverty and inequality; improving the environment and general well-being. So our creed today is progressive Conservatism; and this is an unashamedly progressive Conservative manifesto.

Now we ask you to join us for the next and most important stage of the journey: changing Britain so we can offer a better life to all our citizens and play a proud and leading role in the world.

Each of the three programmes of reform outlined in this manifesto – our plans to build a new economic model; to build the Big Society; to build a political system where people have more power and control over their lives – is a massive undertaking in its own right. Yet we are proposing to carry out these changes all at once, because that is the only way to put Britain on the right path for a successful future.

Britain faces huge problems that demand radical change; and it cannot come soon enough. We are impatient to get on with this work. We are determined to make a difference. We have the policies to make that difference. And most importantly, we have faith in the people of Britain, because we know that if we all pull together, stick together, then this country can change its future.

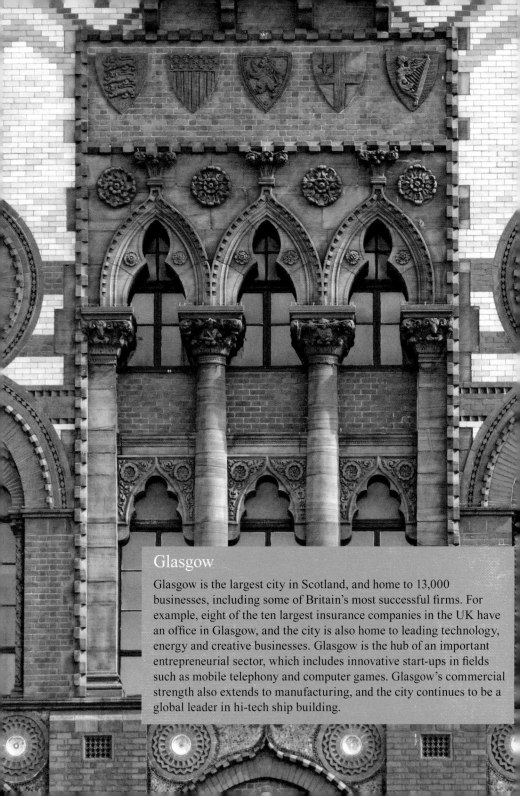

Glasgow

Glasgow is the largest city in Scotland, and home to 13,000 businesses, including some of Britain's most successful firms. For example, eight of the ten largest insurance companies in the UK have an office in Glasgow, and the city is also home to leading technology, energy and creative businesses. Glasgow is the hub of an important entrepreneurial sector, which includes innovative start-ups in fields such as mobile telephony and computer games. Glasgow's commercial strength also extends to manufacturing, and the city continues to be a global leader in hi-tech ship building.

Change the economy

LET'S GET BRITAIN MOVING

Get the economy moving

Gordon Brown's debt, waste and taxes have wrecked the economy and threaten to kill the recovery. A Conservative government will take action now to cut the deficit, stop Labour's jobs tax, help keep mortgage rates low and get the economy moving. We will create a new economic model built on investment and savings, not borrowing and debt.

Where is the growth going to come from? Who will provide jobs for the millions out of work? How will families be able to aspire to a better future? These are the questions being asked about Britain, at home and abroad.

One thing is clear. We can't go on with the old model of an economy built on debt. Irresponsible public spending, an overblown banking sector, and unsustainable consumer borrowing on the back of a housing bubble were the features of an age of irresponsibility that left Britain badly exposed to the economic crisis. Now, with the national debt already doubled and in danger of doubling again, it is this debt – together with the jobs tax that Labour will introduce to help pay for it – that threatens to kill the recovery.

Britain needs a new economic model. Saving and business investment must replace reckless borrowing as the foundation of growth. We need to boost enterprise and develop a low carbon, hi-tech economy. Our exports must grow. We need to get Britain working by creating jobs in the private sector, and we must get better value for money from the public sector.

With the next Conservative government, our tax system, education and national infrastructure will help British firms out-compete their global rivals, not hold them back. We will build a more balanced economy that does not depend so heavily on the success of financial services, and where all parts of the country share in the gains. The bedrock of this new economic model will be the stability and low interest rates that come from a credible plan to reduce our record budget deficit, protect Britain's credit rating and give taxpayers value for their money.

Building this new economic model requires a national effort. We can reverse Britain's economic decline – but only if we accept that we are all in this together. No government, even a strong and united one, can create a better country alone. It needs individuals, families and businesses pulling alongside. We want to unite everyone in our country behind this bold vision of a new British economic model.

GET BRITAIN WORKING

Benchmarks for Britain

For the first time, the British people will have eight clear and transparent benchmarks against which they can judge the economic success or failure of the next government. We will be accountable and open. These are the eight Benchmarks for Britain. Achieving them over the next Parliament will mean we have put Britain back on its feet and are building a new British economic model, very different from the debt-driven economy of recent years.

1. Ensure macroeconomic stability: **We will safeguard Britain's credit rating with a credible plan to eliminate the bulk of the structural deficit over a Parliament. Our fiscal policy will seek to help keep interest rates lower for longer. The independent Bank of England will continue to target 2 per cent Consumer Price Index (CPI) inflation, and will use its new role in prudential supervision to preserve financial stability.**

2. Create a more balanced economy: **We will create the conditions for higher exports, business investment and saving as a share of Gross Domestic Product (GDP).**

3. Get Britain working again: **We will reduce youth unemployment and reduce the number of children in workless households as part of our strategy for tackling poverty and inequality.**

4. Encourage enterprise: **We will improve Britain's international rankings for tax competitiveness and business regulation.**

5. Ensure the whole country shares in rising prosperity: **We will increase the private sector's share of the economy in all regions of the country, especially outside London and the South East.**

6. Reform public services to deliver better value for money: **We will raise productivity growth in the public sector in order to deliver better schools and a better NHS.**

7. Create a safer banking system that serves the needs of the economy: **We will reform the regulation and structure of the banking system to ensure lower levels of leverage, less dependence on unstable wholesale funding, and greater availability of credit for small and medium-sized enterprises (SMEs).**

8. Build a greener economy: **We will reduce UK greenhouse gas emissions and increase our share of global markets for low carbon technologies.**

National debt

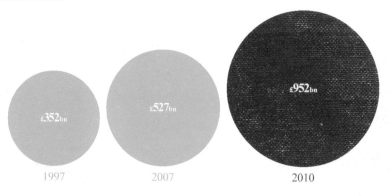

£352bn — 1997
£527bn — 2007
£952bn — 2010

Source: HM Treasury

Budget deficit, 2010, % of GDP

| 3.5% | 5.2% | 5.3% | 5.4% | 8.2% | 8.6% | 10.7% | 11.1% |
| Australia | Canada | Germany | Italy | Japan | France | US | UK |

Source: OECD, HM Treasury

Public spending, 2010

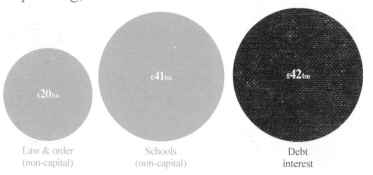

£20bn — Law & order (non-capital)
£41bn — Schools (non-capital)
£42bn — Debt interest

Source: HM Treasury, Department for Children, Schools, and Families

Ensure macroeconomic stability

We will safeguard Britain's credit rating with a credible plan to eliminate the bulk of the structural deficit over a Parliament. Our fiscal policy will help keep interest rates lower for longer. The independent Bank of England will continue to target 2 per cent CPI inflation, and will use its new role in prudential supervision to preserve financial stability.

After a decade of mismanagement, the UK entered the recession in poor shape, with the second biggest budget deficit in the developed world. We have been honest about the scale of the problem, and the actions we will need to take to deal with it. This will not be easy, but we can overcome our problems if we all pull together.

The absence of a credible plan to deal with our record budget deficit, the largest of any major economy, is creating uncertainty over Britain's credit rating and interest rates. This instability undermines confidence and jeopardises investment. It could tip Britain back into recession. This is Gordon Brown's legacy – and why the greatest risk to our economic recovery is five more years of Gordon Brown.

Urgent action to reduce debt

Urgent action is needed if we are to avoid the higher borrowing costs that would inevitably follow from a credit rating downgrade. So we will cut wasteful government spending to bring the deficit down and restore stability.

We will increase spending on health in real terms every year and honour our commitments on international aid, but our plan to get a grip on the deficit will include cuts to wasteful spending in many other departmental budgets. That will enable the independent Bank of England to keep interest rates as low as possible for as long as possible.

To ensure that no Labour government can ever attempt to bankrupt our public finances again, we will set up an independent Office for Budget Responsibility to restore trust in the government's ability to manage the public finances.

We will provide an emergency Budget within 50 days of taking office to set out a credible plan for eliminating the bulk of the structural current budget deficit over a Parliament. The case for starting early to re-establish our economic credibility is overwhelming, and is backed by economists and business leaders.

We will start by cutting a net £6 billion of wasteful departmental spending in the financial year 2010/11. In addition, we will make the following savings:

- freeze public sector pay for one year in 2011, excluding the one million lowest paid workers;

- hold a review to bring forward the date at which the state pension age starts to rise to 66, although it will not be sooner than 2016 for men and 2020 for women;

- stop paying tax credits to better-off families with incomes over £50,000;

- cut government contributions to Child Trust Funds for all but the poorest third of families and families with disabled children;

- cap public sector pensions above £50,000;

- cut Ministers' pay by 5 per cent, followed by a five year freeze; and,

- reduce the number of MPs by 10 per cent.

Over the course of a Parliament, we will cut Whitehall policy, funding and regulation costs by a third, saving £2 billion a year, and save a further £1 billion a year from quango bureaucracy.

Cut government waste to stop Labour's jobs tax

Labour are planning to increase National Insurance in 2011. Anyone earning over £20,000 will pay more tax, and employers will pay more tax on all jobs paid over £5,700. This jobs tax, which will hit small businesses especially hard, will kill off the recovery. Experts predict it will cost 57,000 jobs in small and medium-sized businesses alone.

At the same time, Labour will not take action to cut waste in government. They have identified £11 billion pounds of waste, but they do not plan to start dealing with it until April 2011. So Labour will continue wasting money while putting up taxes on working people.

We will act immediately to cut government waste so we can stop the most damaging part of the National Insurance rise for employers and for anyone earning under £35,000.

We will make the following changes in April 2011, relative to Labour's plans:

- raise the primary threshold for National Insurance by £24 a week and raise the Upper Earnings Limit by £29 a week; and,

- raise the secondary threshold at which employers start paying National Insurance by £21 a week.

Seven out of ten working people – those earning between £7,100 and £45,400 – and almost every employer will save up to £150 a year per person compared to under Labour. Lower earners will get the greatest benefit as a percentage of their earnings. Nobody will be worse off as a result of these changes.

Our plans are backed by many of Britain's top business leaders, who between them employ more than half a million people, as well as by Britain's leading business organisations.

To pay for this we will take immediate action to cut a net £6 billion of wasteful departmental spending in the financial year 2010/11, with further savings in future years. This is in addition to the savings made by cutting tax credits and Child Trust Funds for better-off families.

These actions will allow us to reduce the deficit more quickly than Labour year-on-year while avoiding the most damaging part of their jobs tax. It will also lower the proportion of the reduction of the structural deficit that is accounted for by tax increases, from about one third towards one fifth. This is in line with international best practice, as well as the Treasury's own internal analysis.

Former government advisers Sir Peter Gershon and Dr Martin Read have advised us that savings of £12 billion across all departmental spending are possible in-year without affecting the quality of frontline services. These are over and above any savings already planned by Labour. We will achieve this through:

- a freeze on major new Information and Communications Technologies (ICT) spending;

- immediate negotiations to achieve cost reductions from major suppliers;

- tighter control of public sector recruitment;

- reductions in discretionary spending, including travel, expenses, advertising, consultancy and office supplies; and,

- reductions in public sector property costs.

We will match Labour's spending plans for 2010/11 in health and overseas aid. Given our commitment to carry out a Strategic Defence and Security Review, it would also not be appropriate to make in-year reductions to the existing defence budget in 2010/11. Savings in these protected areas will be channelled back into frontline services. The net £6 billion of savings will be made from the remaining departmental budgets.

Growth in key economic sectors, 1997-2009

Financial services

Housing property

Manufacturing

Source: Office for National Statistics

Create a more balanced economy

We will create the conditions for higher exports, business investment and saving as a share of GDP.

For the last decade, growth has been too dependent on government spending and debt-fuelled consumption. More than half of the new jobs created were driven by public spending. Household savings collapsed, and the UK has the lowest investment as a share of GDP of any G7 country. Our share of world exports has fallen by almost a third. A sustainable recovery must be driven by growth in exports and business investment, and through a better environment for wealth creation.

Make Britain the leading hi-tech exporter in Europe

We will implement key recommendations from Sir James Dyson's Review into how to achieve our goal of making Britain Europe's leading hi-tech exporter, including:

* encouraging the establishment of joint university-business research and development institutes;

* initiating a multi-year Science and Research Budget to provide a stable investment climate for Research Councils;

* creating a better focus on Science, Technology, Engineering and Maths (STEM) subjects in schools; and,

* establishing a new prize for engineering.

Research and development tax credits will be improved and refocused on hi-tech companies, small businesses and new start-ups. At the same time, we will give strong backing to the growth industries that generate high-quality jobs around the country.

We will improve the performance of UK Trade and Investment with a renewed focus on high priority sectors and markets where the return on taxpayers' money is highest. We will regularly compare government support for exporters and inward investment against the services provided by our competitors. We will work for the successful conclusion of the Doha trade round and support bilateral free trade negotiations between the European Union (EU) and other countries.

Encourage saving and investment

Only by saving more can we finance investment for the future without being dependent on unsustainable inflows of capital from abroad. We will help stop the spread of means-testing by restoring the link between the basic state pension and average earnings, making it worthwhile for people to save. Other measures we will take to encourage saving include:

- reinvigorating occupational pensions and working with employers and industry to support auto-enrolment into pensions;

- working with the trade unions, businesses and others to address the growing disparity between public sector pensions and private sector pensions, while protecting accrued rights; and,

- when resources allow, starting to reverse the effects of the abolition of the dividend tax credit for pension funds.

We will reward those who have saved for their retirement by ending the effective obligation to buy an annuity at age 75. And we will raise the inheritance tax threshold to £1 million to help millions of people who aspire to pass something on to their children, paid for by a simple flat-rate levy on all non-domiciled individuals.

We must not let the mis-selling of financial products put people off saving. We will implement the Ombudsman's recommendation to make fair and transparent payments to Equitable Life policy holders, through an independent payment scheme, for their relative loss as a consequence of regulatory failure.

Help households manage their debts

Going into the recession, Britain's consumer debt was the highest in the G7. A Conservative government will promote responsible consumer finance by creating a powerful Consumer Protection Agency (CPA) to take over the Financial Services Authority's consumer protection role. In addition, we will:

- give the CPA new powers to define and ban excessive borrowing rates on store cards;

- launch Britain's first free national financial advice service, funded in full through a new social responsibility levy on the financial services sector;

- introduce a seven-day cooling off period for store cards;

- require credit card companies to provide clear information; and,

- ensure that no-one is forced to sell their home to pay unsecured debts of less than £25,000.

Debbie Scott

"I've always believed that we'll only solve our big social and economic problems if we all get involved and try and make a difference. It's never enough just to sit back and think 'well the government can take care of it' – I think we've all got a responsibility to do what we can. That's why every day, my colleagues and I use all the innovation and flexibility we can muster to help those furthest from the labour market to overcome their personal barriers to work. For me, it is all about believing in the power of people. Tomorrow's People welcomes the concept of the single Work Programme – it pulls everything together and allows organisations like ours to support people more effectively on their individual journey from welfare into work."

Debbie Scott is the Chief Executive of Tomorrow's People, a national employment charity founded in 1984

Get Britain working again

We will reduce youth unemployment and reduce the number of children in workless households as part of our strategy for tackling poverty and inequality.

Under Labour, youth unemployment has reached over 900,000, with one in five young people unable to find a job. We are at risk of creating a lost generation of young people without the skills to participate in the workforce, without hope for the future. At the same time, economic inactivity is rising, and more than five million people are out of work and on benefits.

This tidal wave of worklessness is making it hard for many families to make ends meet. In recent years, the number of people living in severe poverty has risen. One in six children in the UK now lives in a workless household – the highest proportion of any country in Europe – and child poverty has gone up in recent years. Getting people back into work is an essential part of realising the goal of eliminating child poverty by 2020, and ensuring that everyone benefits from economic growth.

Reduce welfare dependency

We will scrap Labour's failing employment schemes and create a single Work Programme for everyone who is unemployed, including the 2.6 million people claiming Incapacity Benefit who do not get enough help from existing programmes. We will reassess all current claimants of Incapacity Benefit. Those found fit for work will be transferred onto Jobseeker's Allowance. Recipients of Incapacity Benefit who are genuinely disabled will continue to receive the financial support to which they are entitled. Our Work Programme will:

- offer people targeted, personalised help sooner – straight away for those with serious barriers to work and at six months for those aged under 25;

- be delivered through private and voluntary sector providers, which will be rewarded on a payment by results basis for getting people into sustainable work;

- draw on a range of Service Academies to offer pre-employment training for unemployed people – our first Service Academy, for hospitality and leisure, will provide up to 50,000 training places and work placements; and,

- involve the development of local Work Clubs – places where people looking for work can gather together to exchange skills, find opportunities, make useful contacts and provide mutual support.

Our plans will give unemployed people a hand up, not a hand out. Unemployed people must be prepared to take up job offers. So, with the Conservatives, long-term benefit claimants who fail to find work will be required to 'work for the dole' on community work programmes. Anyone on Jobseeker's Allowance who refuses to join the Work Programme will lose the right to claim out-of-work benefits until they do, while people who refuse to accept reasonable job offers could forfeit their benefits for up to three years. This will create a welfare system that is fair but firm.

Boost small business

In the end, it is not the state that creates sustainable employment – it is business people. And small businesses are especially important to the UK's economic recovery and to tackling unemployment. Government can help boost enterprise by lowering tax rates, reducing regulation and improving workers' skills.

As well as stopping Labour's jobs tax, for the first two years of a Conservative government any new business will pay no Employers National Insurance on the first ten employees it hires during its first year.

To support small businesses further, we will:

- make small business rate relief automatic; and,

- aim to deliver 25 per cent of government research and procurement contracts through SMEs by cutting the administrative costs of bidding.

We will support would-be entrepreneurs through a new programme – Work for Yourself – which will give unemployed people direct access to business mentors and substantial loans. We need to make work pay, so we will keep the minimum wage and work to reduce the very high marginal tax rates faced by many people on low incomes who want to return to work or increase their earnings. We will look at how to abolish the default retirement age, as many older people want to carry on working. And we will force equal pay audits on any company found to be discriminating on the basis of gender.

Improve skills and strengthen higher education

Developing economies are able to provide highly-skilled work at a fraction of the cost of British labour. The only way we can compete is by dramatically improving the skills of Britain's workforce, yet thousands of young people leave school every year without the skills they need to get a good job. A Conservative government will not accept another generation being consigned to an uncertain future of worklessness and dependency.

We will promote fair access to universities, the professions, and good jobs for young people from all backgrounds. We will use funding that currently supports Labour's ineffective employment and training schemes, such as Train2Gain, to provide our own help for people looking to improve their skills. This will allow us to:

- create 400,000 work pairing, apprenticeship, college and training places over two years;

- give SMEs a £2,000 bonus for every apprentice they hire;

- establish a Community Learning Fund to help people restart their careers; and,

- create a new all-age careers service so that everyone can access the advice they need.

To meet the skills challenge we face, the training sector needs to be given the freedom to innovate. We will set colleges free from direct state control and abolish many of the further education quangos Labour have put in place. Public funding will follow the choices of students and be delivered by a single agency, the Further Education Funding Council.

Universities contribute enormously to the economy. But not all of this contribution comes directly – it can come from fundamental research with no immediate application – and universities also have a crucial cultural role. We will ensure that Britain's universities enjoy the freedom to pursue academic excellence and focus on raising the quality of the student experience. To enable this to happen, we will:

- delay the implementation of the Research Excellence Framework so that it can be reviewed – because of doubts about whether there is a robust and acceptable way of measuring the impact of all research;

- consider carefully the results of Lord Browne's review into the future of higher education funding, so that we can unlock the potential of universities to transform our economy, to enrich students' lives through teaching of the highest quality, and to advance scholarship; and,

- provide 10,000 extra university places this year, paid for by giving graduates incentives to pay back their student loans early on an entirely voluntary basis.

Silicon Valley

Despite having a population twenty times smaller than the UK, Silicon Valley is a global beacon for innovation and enterprise, attracting more venture capital investment than the whole of the UK. Having led the internet revolution, Silicon Valley is now becoming a world leader in green technology development. These successes are thanks to the highly skilled workforce and world-class universities, the ease of starting a business, and the availability of credit and investment. In addition, companies in Silicon Valley have been able to attract employees in a highly competitive labour market by introducing measures to improve the general well-being of their staff, including flexible working and childcare facilities.

Encourage enterprise

We will improve Britain's international rankings for tax competitiveness and business regulation.

Thirteen years ago, Britain's tax system was one of the most competitive in the developed world. Over the last decade, other countries have cut their tax rates while our tax system has become one of the most complex in the world. Our competitiveness rating has fallen, while the burden of regulation and the impact of taxation have risen. We can only make a sustainable economic recovery if we send a clear signal that Britain is open for business again. That means stopping Labour's jobs tax, lowering corporate tax rates, reducing the regulatory burden, and supporting innovation and sustainable development – changes that will benefit businesses of all sizes and boost employment.

Cut and simplify business taxes

The Conservative Party believes in lower and simpler taxation. That is why we will ensure that by far the largest part of the burden of dealing with the deficit falls on lower spending rather than higher taxes. Cutting the deficit is the most urgent task we need to undertake if we are to get the economy moving, but it is not enough. So, initially, we will cut the headline rate of corporation tax to 25p and the small companies' rate to 20p, funded by reducing complex reliefs and allowances.

Over time, we hope to reduce these rates further. Our ambition is to create the most competitive tax system in the G20 within five years.

We will restore the tax system's reputation for simplicity, stability and predictability. In our first Budget, we will set out a five year road map for the direction of corporate tax reform, providing greater certainty and stability to businesses. We will create an independent Office of Tax Simplification to suggest reforms to the tax system.

We will take a series of measures to encourage Foreign Direct Investment into the UK, including:

- making the UK a more attractive location for multinationals by simplifying the complex Controlled Foreign Companies rules;

- consulting on moving towards a territorial corporate tax system that only taxes profits generated in the UK; and,

- creating an attractive tax environment for intellectual property.

Reduce regulation

Increasing amounts of red tape and complex regulation have eroded Britain's reputation as a good place to invest, create jobs or start a business. A Conservative government will introduce regulatory budgets: forcing any government body wanting to introduce a new regulation to reduce regulation elsewhere by a greater amount. And we will give the public the opportunity to force the worst regulations to be repealed.

To encourage new businesses to start up, we will reduce the number of forms needed to register a new business – moving towards a 'one-click' registration model – to make Britain the fastest place in the world to start a business, and end the restrictions on social tenants starting a business from their homes.

We are proud of the last Conservative government's industrial relations reforms, which helped bring about our economic revival in the 1980s, and we will always be prepared to build on them if necessary.

Support innovation and sustainable development

Government procurement is a £200 billion a year market that can be used much better to stimulate enterprise and innovation. We will take steps to open up government procurement to small and innovative businesses by:

- publishing online all government tender documents for contracts worth over £10,000 via the Supply2Gov website;

- creating a level playing field for open source ICT in government procurement; and,

- opening up contracts to SMEs by breaking up large ICT projects into smaller components.

Britain's complex and unwieldy planning system has long been cited as a significant barrier to growth and wealth creation. We will create a presumption in favour of sustainable development in the planning system. We will abolish the unelected Infrastructure Planning Commission (IPC) and replace it with an efficient and democratically-accountable system that provides a fast-track process for major infrastructure projects. We will:

- use private or hybrid Bills to promote major projects, such as our plans for a national high speed rail network;

- ensure that all other major infrastructure projects are considered at planning inquiries which have binding timetables and which focus on planning issues – with final permission given by a Minister; and,

- provide transitional arrangements for projects already before the IPC to ensure that these projects are not disrupted or delayed.

Attract the brightest and best to our country

Immigration has enriched our nation over the years and we want to attract the brightest and the best people who can make a real difference to our economic growth. But immigration today is too high and needs to be reduced. We do not need to attract people to do jobs that could be carried out by British citizens, given the right training and support. So we will take steps to take net migration back to the levels of the 1990s – tens of thousands a year, not hundreds of thousands.

To help achieve this goal, we will introduce a number of measures, such as:

* setting an annual limit on the number of non-EU economic migrants admitted into the UK to live and work;

* limiting access only to those who will bring the most value to the British economy; and,

* applying transitional controls as a matter of course in the future for all new EU Member States.

In addition, we will promote integration into British society, as we believe that everyone coming to this country must be ready to embrace our core values and become a part of their local community. So there will be an English language test for anyone coming here to get married.

We want to encourage students to come to our universities and colleges, but our student visa system has become the biggest weakness in our border controls. A Conservative government will strengthen the system of granting student visas so that it is less open to abuse. We want to make it easier for reputable universities and colleges to accept applications, while putting extra scrutiny on new institutions looking to accept foreign students or existing institutions not registered with Companies House. In addition, we will:

* insist foreign students at new or unregistered institutions pay a bond in order to study in this country, to be repaid after the student has left the country at the end of their studies;

* ensure foreign students can prove that they have the financial means to support themselves in the UK; and,

* require that students must usually leave the country and reapply if they want to switch to another course or apply for a work permit.

Country or region size by share of UK economy

Source: Office for National Statistics, 2008

Ensure the whole country shares in rising prosperity

We will increase the private sector's share of the economy in all regions of the country, especially outside London and the South East.

Too many areas of the UK lack a vibrant private sector and are too dependent on public spending. These regional imbalances have got worse over the last decade, despite billions of pounds spent by the Regional Development Agencies (RDAs). Our aim is to increase the private sector's share of the economy in every part of the country by boosting enterprise and creating a better business environment. We will work closely with local government, and with the Scottish Parliament, Welsh Assembly and Northern Ireland Assembly, to achieve this goal.

Create a modern transport network

A rebalanced economy requires an extensive and reliable infrastructure. But transport has been a low priority for Labour, and the hassle of getting around is bad for business, bad for families and bad for everyone's quality of life.

A Conservative government will begin work immediately to create a high speed rail line connecting London and Heathrow with Birmingham, Manchester and Leeds. This is the first step towards achieving our vision of creating a national high speed rail network to join up major cities across England, Scotland and Wales. Stage two will deliver two new lines bringing the North East, Scotland and Wales into the high speed rail network.

Because travel abroad is so important for our economy and for family holidays, we need to improve our airports and reduce the environmental impact of flying. Our goal is to make Heathrow airport better, not bigger. We will stop the third runway and instead link Heathrow directly to our high speed rail network, providing an alternative to thousands of flights. In addition, we will:

- block plans for second runways at Stansted and Gatwick; and,

- reform Air Passenger Duty to encourage a switch to fuller and cleaner planes.

To improve life for commuters and encourage people to switch to lower carbon public transport, we will reform our railways to provide a better focus on tackling problems that matter most to passengers, such as overcrowding. We will grant longer, more flexible rail franchises to incentivise private sector investment in improvements like longer trains and better stations.

We support Crossrail and the electrification of the Great Western line to South Wales. We will turn the rail regulator into a powerful passenger champion and reform Network Rail to make it more accountable to its customers. And we will introduce a moratorium on building on disused rail lines still in public ownership, so they are available to be re-opened.

Britain has the chance to lead the world in making our transport system greener. So we will introduce incentives for electricity network operators to establish a new national car recharging network, making it much easier for drivers to move to electric and plug-in hybrid vehicles. We will support sustainable travel initiatives that work best for local communities by:

- giving the concerns of cyclists much greater priority;

- encouraging partnerships between bus operators and local authorities; and,

- helping people cut down on work-related travel.

We will stop central government funding for new fixed speed cameras, and switch to more effective ways to make our roads safer, including authorising 'drugalyser' technology for use in testing for drug-driving. We will make companies that dig up our roads accountable for the congestion they cause and crack down on rogue clampers. Councils will get more powers to get traffic flowing more smoothly.

We will consult on the introduction of a 'Fair Fuel Stabiliser'. This would cut fuel duty when oil prices rise, and vice versa. It would ensure families, businesses and the whole British economy are less exposed to volatile oil markets, and that there is a more stable environment for low carbon investment.

Spread prosperity

We want Britain to become a European hub for hi-tech, digital and creative industries – but this can only happen if we have the right infrastructure in place. Establishing a super-fast broadband network throughout the UK could generate 600,000 additional jobs and add £18 billion to Britain's GDP.

We will scrap Labour's phone tax and instead require BT and other infrastructure providers to allow the use of their assets to deliver super-fast broadband across the country. If necessary, we will consider using the part of the licence fee that is supporting the digital switchover to fund broadband in areas that the market alone will not reach.

We will give councils and businesses the power to form their own business-led local enterprise partnerships instead of RDAs. Where local councils and businesses want to maintain regionally-based enterprise partnerships, they will be able to. Local government should be at the heart of our economic recovery, so we will:

- allow councils to keep above-average increases in business rate revenue so that communities which go for growth can reap the benefits;

- give councils new powers to introduce further discounts on business rates; and,

- introduce an immediate freeze of, and inquiry into, the Government's punitive programme of back-dating business rates on ports.

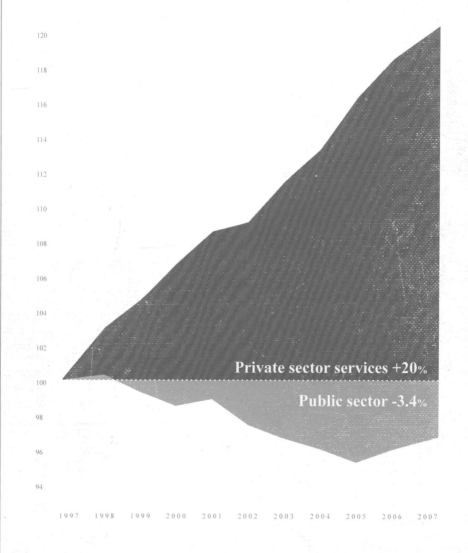

Productivity, 1997-2007

120

118

116

114

112

110

108

106

104

102

100

98

96

94

Private sector services +20%

Public sector -3.4%

1997   1998   1999   2000   2001   2002   2003   2004   2005   2006   2007

Source: Office for National Statistics

Reform public services to deliver better value for money

We will raise productivity growth in the public sector in order to deliver better schools and a better NHS.

Public sector productivity has fallen under Labour, acting as a drag on growth and reducing the quality of our public services. If productivity in the public sector had grown at the same rate as in private sector services, we could now have the same quality of public services for £60 billion less each year. So, by improving public sector productivity while getting a grip on the debt, we will still be able to deliver better public services. That is why good government costs less with the Conservatives.

Decentralisation, accountability and transparency

We value the work of those employed in our public services, and a Conservative government will work with them to deliver higher productivity and better value for money for taxpayers. We will raise public sector productivity by increasing diversity of provision, extending payment by results and giving more power to consumers.

Giving public sector workers ownership of the services they deliver is a powerful way to drive efficiency, so we will support co-operatives and mutualisation as a way of transferring public assets and revenue streams to public sector workers. We will encourage them to come together to form employee-led co-operatives and bid to take over the services they run. This will empower millions of public sector workers to become their own boss and help them to deliver better services – the most significant shift in power from the state to working people since the sale of council houses in the 1980s.

Transparency is crucial to creating a value for money culture. We will publish all items of spending over £25,000 online, and the salaries of senior civil servants in central government will also be published. We will create strong financial discipline at all levels of government and place an obligation to manage taxpayers' money wisely at the heart of civil service employment contracts. In addition, we will:

- introduce and publish a standard set of cost measures that capture the key drivers of departmental spending;

- help departmental Finance Directors to manage resources more efficiently;

- implement clear financial performance targets for senior civil servants; and,

- create a focus on delivering strong financial management across government.

Size of peak bank bailout, % GDP

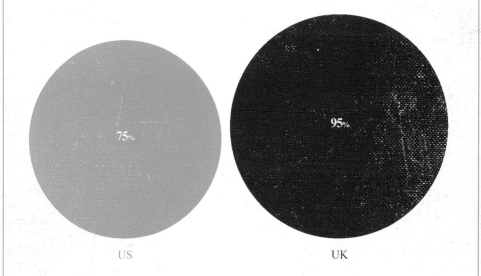

75%

95%

US

UK

Source: Bank of England

Create a safer banking system that serves the needs of the economy

We will reform the regulation and structure of the banking system to ensure lower levels of leverage, less dependence on unstable wholesale funding, and greater availability of credit for SMEs.

In the run up to the financial crisis, British banks became amongst the most indebted and most leveraged in the world – with disastrous consequences for us all. This credit boom turned into a bust, with a significant fall in credit available to firms. Lack of access to credit remains a major problem, especially for SMEs. We need to change the way we regulate our banks to stop a crisis on this scale ever happening again.

Reform financial services

The financial services sector is one of our most globally successful industries, and we want the City to be the leading location for global finance. But the financial sector must not put the stability of the whole economy at risk.

We will put in place a levy on banks. We are prepared to act unilaterally if necessary, but there is emerging international agreement on this approach and the US and German governments have both announced similar plans.

We need fundamental reform of our failed regulatory system, avoiding badly-designed regulations that will damage our competitiveness and ensuring that the financial sector can supply the affordable credit that businesses need.

We will abolish Gordon Brown's failed tripartite system of regulation and put the Bank of England in charge of prudential supervision. We will restore the Bank's historic role in monitoring the overall growth of credit and debt in the economy. In addition, we will:

- pursue international agreement to prevent retail banks from engaging in activities, such as large-scale proprietary trading, that put the stability of the system at risk;

- empower the Bank of England to crack down on risky bonus arrangements;

- increase competition in the banking industry, starting with a study of competition in the sector to inform our strategy for selling the government's stakes in the banks; and,

- as the government comes to sell off its holdings in the banks, offer a 'people's bank bonus', so that everybody in the country has the chance to buy a stake in the state-owned banks.

We will create more diverse sources of affordable credit for small businesses, building on our proposals for a National Loan Guarantee Scheme.

Japan

Japan is a world leader in the development of green technology. It invests in R&D at almost double the UK's rate, and Japanese companies hold roughly 30 per cent of green technology patents filed in the US. As a result, Japan is far ahead of the UK in the trillion pound market for green technology. This leadership is not just good for the economy; it's also good for the environment. For example, thanks to the widespread use of green technologies, Japan has the lowest carbon intensity of any major economy.

Build a greener economy

We will reduce UK greenhouse gas emissions and increase our share of global markets for low carbon technologies.

Labour have said the right things on climate change, but these have proved little more than warm words. Despite three White Papers, a multitude of strategies and endless new announcements, the UK now gets more of its energy from fossil fuels than it did in 1997. Our performance on emissions has been criticised by environmental groups and we have the worst record of any major EU nation when it comes to renewable energy. This must change to safeguard Britain and the world's future.

We need to cut our carbon emissions to tackle the challenge of climate change. But the low carbon economy also provides exciting opportunities for British businesses. We will encourage private sector investment to put Britain at the forefront of the green technology revolution, creating jobs and new businesses across the country.

Create a low carbon future

This wave of low carbon innovation we want to unleash requires investment, so we will create Britain's first Green Investment Bank – which will draw together money currently divided across existing government initiatives, leveraging private sector capital to finance new green technology start-ups. We will create green Individual Savings Accounts to help provide the financial backing we need to create a low carbon economy.

A credible and sustainable price for carbon is vital if we are to see adequate and timely investment in new electricity generation. Whatever the carbon content of electricity generated, operators considering new investments in projects with a life of several decades need to know where they stand. We will reform the Climate Change Levy to provide a floor price for carbon, delivering the right climate for investment in low carbon energy production.

We will increase the proportion of tax revenues accounted for by environmental taxes, ensuring that any additional revenues from new green taxes that are principally designed as an environmental measure to change behaviour are used to reduce the burden of taxation elsewhere.

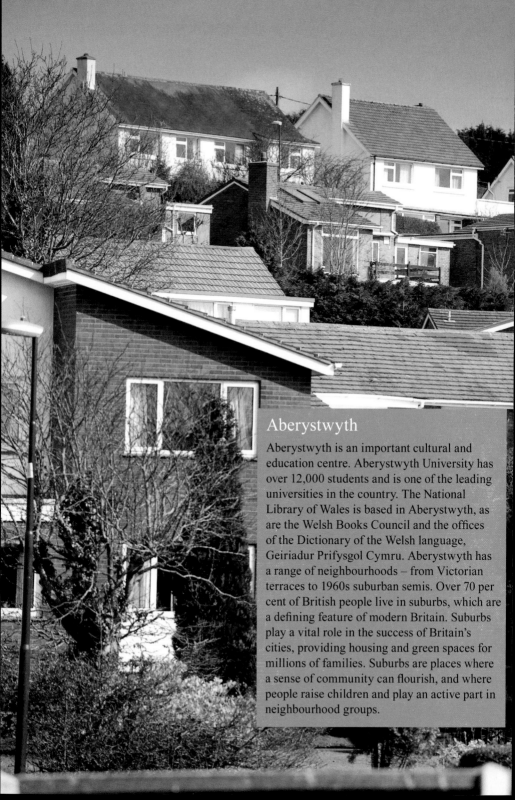

Aberystwyth

Aberystwyth is an important cultural and education centre. Aberystwyth University has over 12,000 students and is one of the leading universities in the country. The National Library of Wales is based in Aberystwyth, as are the Welsh Books Council and the offices of the Dictionary of the Welsh language, Geiriadur Prifysgol Cymru. Aberystwyth has a range of neighbourhoods – from Victorian terraces to 1960s suburban semis. Over 70 per cent of British people live in suburbs, which are a defining feature of modern Britain. Suburbs play a vital role in the success of Britain's cities, providing housing and green spaces for millions of families. Suburbs are places where a sense of community can flourish, and where people raise children and play an active part in neighbourhood groups.

Change society

THERE IS SUCH A THING AS SOCIETY

IT'S JUST NOT THE SAME THING AS THE STATE

Mend our broken society

Our society is broken, but together we can mend it: we can build the Big Society. A Conservative government will make Britain the most family-friendly country in Europe. We will back the NHS, which matters more to families than anything. We will reform education, with new schools – and higher standards and improved discipline for all. We will tackle welfare dependency and the causes of poverty, and fight back against crime.

Despite Labour's massive expansion of the state, many people's quality of life is getting worse, not better. The number of people living in poverty has risen in the last three years, and inequality is at a record high. We have some of the worst rates of family breakdown in the world. In some of the most deprived parts of the country, life expectancy has actually fallen. The achievement gap at school between the richest and poorest is growing.

This terrible record of failure is not just a problem that affects our society and ruins people's lives. It affects our economy too, costing billions and wasting potential. It is the result of a political approach that addresses the symptoms, rather than the underlying causes, of social breakdown; one that relies on top-down government intervention and bureaucratic micro-management.

So we need a new approach: social responsibility, not state control; the Big Society, not big government. Only in this way will we tackle the causes of poverty and inequality, rather than just the symptoms. Only in this way will we transform the quality of our public services. And only in this way will we rebuild shattered communities and repair the torn fabric of society.

So we will redistribute power from the central state to individuals, families and local communities. We will give public sector workers back their professional autonomy. They will be accountable to the people they serve and the results they achieve will be made transparent. If people don't like the service they receive they will be able to choose better alternatives. In this way, we will create opportunities for people to take power and control over their lives. Our approach is absolutely in line with the spirit of the age: the post-bureaucratic age.

This vision demands a cultural change across the country. Our success will depend not just on the actions we take but on society's response. By promoting equality and tackling discrimination, our policies, like recognising civil partnerships as well as marriage in the tax system and helping disabled people live independently, will give everybody the chance to play their part. This way, we can make Britain fairer and safer; a country where opportunity is more equal.

BIG SOCIETY

NOT BIG GOVERNMENT

Build the Big Society

We will use the state to help stimulate social action, helping social enterprises to deliver public services and training new community organisers to help achieve our ambition of every adult citizen being a member of an active neighbourhood group. We will direct funding to those groups that strengthen communities in deprived areas, and we will introduce National Citizen Service, initially for 16 year olds, to help bring our country together.

The size, scope and role of government in the UK has reached a point where it is now inhibiting, not advancing, the progressive aims of reducing poverty, fighting inequality, and increasing general well-being. We can't go on pretending that government has all the answers.

Our alternative to big government is the Big Society: a society with much higher levels of personal, professional, civic and corporate responsibility; a society where people come together to solve problems and improve life for themselves and their communities; a society where the leading force for progress is social responsibility, not state control.

The Big Society runs consistently through our policy programme. Our plans to reform public services, mend our broken society, and rebuild trust in politics are all part of our Big Society agenda. These plans involve redistributing power from the state to society; from the centre to local communities, giving people the opportunity to take more control over their lives.

But we recognise that it is not enough to create opportunities for people to get involved in building the Big Society; our reform plans require a social response in order to be successful. So building the Big Society is not just a question of the state stepping back and hoping for the best: it will require an active role for the state. The state must take action to agitate for, catalyse and galvanise social renewal. We must use the state to help remake society.

Public service reform

Our public service reform programme will enable social enterprises, charities and voluntary groups to play a leading role in delivering public services and tackling deep-rooted social problems.

We will strengthen and support social enterprises to help deliver our public service reforms by creating a Big Society Bank, funded from unclaimed bank assets, to provide new finance for neighbourhood groups, charities, social enterprises and other non-governmental bodies.

This will provide social enterprises with the start-up funding and support they need to bid for government contracts or work towards delivering services under a payment by results model.

Britain has a proud and long-standing charitable tradition, and we are convinced that the voluntary sector should play a major part in our civic renewal. We will introduce a fair deal on grants to give voluntary sector organisations more stability and allow them to earn a competitive return for providing public services. We will work with local authorities to promote the delivery of public services by social enterprises, charities and the voluntary sector.

Neighbourhood groups

Our reform agenda is designed to empower communities to come together to address local issues. For example, we will enable parents to start new schools, empower communities to take over local amenities such as parks and libraries that are under threat, give neighbourhoods greater control of the planning system, and enable residents to hold the police to account in neighbourhood beat meetings. These policies will give new powers and rights to neighbourhood groups: the 'little platoons' of civil society – and the institutional building blocks of the Big Society.

Our ambition is for every adult in the country to be a member of an active neighbourhood group. We will stimulate the creation and development of neighbourhood groups, which can take action to improve their local area. We will use Cabinet Office budgets to fund the training of independent community organisers to help people establish and run neighbourhood groups, and provide neighbourhood grants to the UK's poorest areas to ensure they play a leading role in the rebuilding of civic society.

To stimulate social action further, we will:

- transform the civil service into a 'civic service' by making sure that participation in social action is recognised in civil servants' appraisals;

- launch an annual Big Society Day to celebrate the work of neighbourhood groups and encourage more people to take part in social action;

- provide funding from the Big Society Bank to intermediary bodies with a track record of supporting and growing social enterprises; and,

- develop a measure of well-being that encapsulates the social value of state action.

National Citizen Service

Building the Big Society means encouraging the concept of public-spirited service – the idea that everyone should play a part in making their communities stronger.

That is why we will introduce National Citizen Service. The initial flagship project will provide a programme for 16 year olds to give them a chance to develop the skills needed to be active and responsible citizens, mix with people from different backgrounds, and start getting involved in their communities.

Even in these difficult times, the British people have demonstrated their desire to give money and time to good causes. We will introduce new ways to increase philanthropy, and use the latest insights from behavioural economics to encourage people to make volunteering and community participation something they do on a regular basis.

The National Lottery

We will restore the National Lottery to its original purpose and, by cutting down on administration costs, make sure more money goes to good causes. The Big Lottery Fund will focus purely on supporting social action through the voluntary and community sector, instead of Ministers' pet projects as at present. Sports, heritage and the arts will each see their original allocations of 20 per cent of good cause money restored.

Sport and the Olympics

We will deliver a successful Olympics that brings lasting benefits for the country as a whole. Part of the community sports budget of the National Lottery will be responsible for delivering an Olympic legacy, including the vigorous promotion of competitive sports through a national Olympic-style school competition. To support high-level sport further, we will:

• work with the Scottish government to deliver a top-quality Commonwealth Games in Glasgow in 2014;

• ensure that the 2013 Rugby League and the 2015 Rugby Union World Cups are successful; and,

• strongly support England's bid to host the 2018 Football World Cup.

Julie Fallon

"I went to a 'Cameron Direct' meeting in our local town hall where David Cameron answered questions from members of the public – and one thing he said that really took hold with me was that he wanted Britain to be one of the most family-friendly countries… I think that's just a great outlook to have – how brilliant would it be if we could achieve that? I think that the Tories have some great ideas and I believe that their policies on family, especially on flexible working, are the best thing for my future and for my children's future."

Julie Fallon lives in Llandudno, Wales, with her husband and two children

Make Britain the most family-friendly country in Europe

We will make Britain the most family-friendly country in Europe. We will support families in the tax and benefits system, extend flexible working and improve parental leave. We will help parents cope with the commercialisation of childhood and give families more control over their lives. We will support and improve Sure Start, and introduce a new universal health visiting service. We will give targeted help to disadvantaged and dysfunctional families.

Strong families are the bedrock of a strong society. They provide the stability and love we need to flourish as human beings, and the relationships they foster are the foundation on which society is built. The warmth of a child's parenting is as important to their life chances as the wealth of their upbringing.

Labour's complacent attitude to commitment has done untold harm, and their narrow approach ignores the importance of strengthening the relationships between all family members – children, parents, grandparents and the wider family. As a result, Britain is one of the least family-friendly countries in the world.

This will change with a Conservative government. We will help families with all the pressures they face: the lack of time, money worries, the impact of work, concerns about schools and crime, preventing unhealthy influences, poor housing. We will not be neutral on this. Britain's families will get our full backing across all our policies.

Reform tax and benefits to help families and pensioners

Today, Labour's tax and benefits system rewards couples who split up. A Conservative government will end the couple penalty for all couples in the tax credit system as we make savings from our welfare reform plans. We will recognise marriage and civil partnerships in the tax system in the next Parliament. This will send an important signal that we value couples and the commitment that people make when they get married.

To help Britain's families further, a Conservative government will freeze council tax for two years, in partnership with local councils. This will be paid for by reducing spending on government consultants and advertising, and could save families and pensioners up to £219 over two years on a Band D bill. We will also scrap Labour's plans for an expensive and intrusive council tax revaluation.

We support tax credits and will continue to provide the range of tax credits to families, although we can no longer justify paying tax credits to households earning more than £50,000. We will reform the administration of tax credits to reduce fraud and overpayments, which hit the poorest families hardest.

We strongly value the role older people play in families and in society, and will not let them suffer because of the economic mistakes of others. That is why we have made a pledge to pensioners to re-link the basic state pension to earnings, and protect:

- the winter fuel payment;

- free bus passes;

- free TV licences;

- disability living allowance and attendance allowance; and,

- the pension credit.

Give families more control over their lives

Making Britain more family-friendly means helping families spend more time together. That is why we will initially extend the right to request flexible working to every parent with a child under the age of eighteen. We want our government to lead from the front, so we will extend the right to request flexible working to all those in the public sector, recognising that

this may need to be done in stages. In addition, we will:

- in the longer term, extend the right to request flexible working to all, but only in the light of experience and after full consultation with business on how to do this in a way which is administratively simple and without burdening them with extra costs; and,

- oblige JobCentre Plus offices to ask employers if their vacancies could be advertised on a part-time or flexible basis.

We will introduce a new system of flexible parental leave which lets parents share maternity leave between them, while ensuring that parents on leave can stay in touch with their employer. We support the provision of free nursery care for pre-school children, and we want that support to be provided by a diverse range of providers. A Conservative government will review the way the childcare industry is regulated and funded to ensure that no providers, including childminders, are put at a disadvantage.

To give families more control over their lives, we will put funding for relationship support on a stable, long-term footing and make sure couples are given greater encouragement to use existing relationship support. We will review family law in order to increase the use of mediation when couples do break up, and look at how best to provide greater access rights to non-resident parents and grandparents.

Protect childhood

Children should be allowed to grow up at their own pace, without excessive pressure placed on them by businesses. We will take a series of measures to help reverse the commercialisation of childhood. We prefer to gain voluntary consent to these actions but we are prepared to legislate if necessary. We will:

- prevent any marketing or advertising company found to be in serious breach of rules governing marketing to children from bidding for government advertising contracts for three years;

- ban companies from using new peer-to-peer marketing techniques targeted at children, and tackle marketing on corporate websites targeted at children;

- establish a new online system that gives parents greater powers to take action against irresponsible commercial activities targeted at children; and,

- empower head teachers and governors to ban advertising and vending machines in schools.

A new approach to early intervention

The Conservative Party is committed to keeping Sure Start because the network of Children's Centres is of enormous value to parents across the country. But we believe Sure Start needs to work better because the people who need it most – disadvantaged and dysfunctional families – are not getting enough of the benefit.

We will take Sure Start back to its original purpose of early intervention, increase its focus on the neediest families, and better involve organisations with a track record in supporting families.

Families need the best possible advice and support while their children are young. We will provide 4,200 more Sure Start health visitors – giving all parents a guaranteed level of support before and after birth until their child starts school. This will be paid for out of the Department of Health budget and by refocusing Sure Start's peripatetic outreach services.

To improve the early interventions we make to help families, we will:

- ensure that new Sure Start providers are paid in part by the results they achieve;

- bring all funding for early intervention and parenting support into one budget, to be overseen by a single, newly-created Early Years Support Team; and,

- set out a new approach to help families with multiple problems.

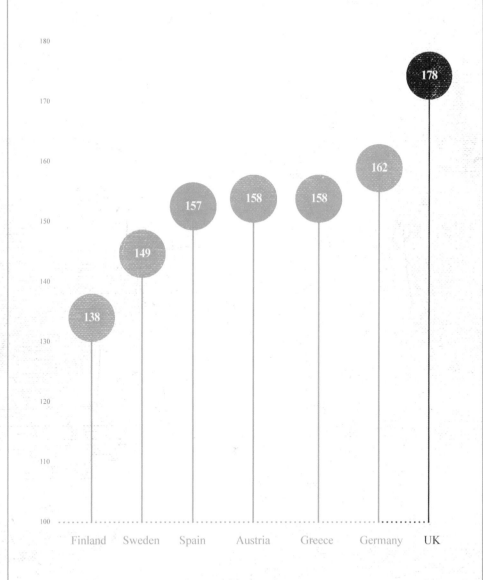

Deaths due to cancer, per 100,000 people

138	149	157	158	158	162	178
Finland	Sweden	Spain	Austria	Greece	Germany	UK

Source: EuroStat, 2007

Back the NHS

We will back the NHS. We will increase health spending every year. We will give patients more choice and free health professionals from the tangle of politically-motivated targets that get in the way of providing the best care. We will give patients better access to the treatments, services and information that improve and extend lives, boost the nation's health, and reform social care.

More than three years ago, David Cameron spelled out his priorities in three letters – NHS. Since then, we have consistently fought to protect the values the NHS stands for and have campaigned to defend the NHS from Labour's cuts and reorganisations. As the party of the NHS, we will never change the idea at its heart – that healthcare in this country is free at the point of use and available to everyone based on need, not ability to pay.

We have a reform plan to make the changes the NHS needs. We will decentralise power, so that patients have a real choice. We will make doctors and nurses accountable to patients, not to endless layers of bureaucracy and management. We can't go on with an NHS that puts targets before patients.

We will make the performance of the NHS totally transparent by publishing information about the kind of results that healthcare providers are achieving, so there is no hiding place for failure. We will increase access to vital drugs and services, and create a greater focus on preventing people getting ill in the first place. This is how we will achieve our ambition for the NHS to deliver some of the best healthcare in the world.

We are the party of the NHS today because we not only back the values of the NHS, we back its funding and have a vision for its future.

Give patients more choice

We understand the pressures the NHS faces, so we will increase health spending in real terms every year. But on its own this will not be enough to deliver the rising standards of care that people expect. We need to allow patients to choose the best care available, giving healthcare providers the incentives they need to drive up quality.

So we will give every patient the power to choose any healthcare provider that meets NHS standards, within NHS prices. This includes independent, voluntary and community sector providers. We will make patients' choices meaningful by:

- putting patients in charge of making decisions about their care, including control of their health records;

- spreading the use of the NHS tariff, so funding follows patients' choices; and,

- making sure good performance is rewarded by implementing a payment by results system, improving quality.

We will publish detailed data about the performance of healthcare providers online, so everyone will know who is providing a good service and who is falling behind, and we will measure our success on the health results that really matter – such as improving cancer and stroke survival rates or reducing hospital infections.

Patients will be able to rate hospitals and doctors according to the quality of care they received. We will give the public a strong and independent voice through HealthWatch, a statutory body with the power to investigate and support complaints.

We will strengthen the power of GPs as patients' expert guides through the health system by:

- giving them the power to hold patients' budgets and commission care on their behalf;

- linking their pay to the quality of their results; and,

- putting them in charge of commissioning local health services.

Trust healthcare professionals

Doctors and nurses need to be able to use their professional judgement about what is right for patients, instead of being forced to follow bureaucratic processes that often put lives at risk. That is why we will scrap the politically-motivated targets that have no clinical justification. We will set NHS providers free to innovate by ensuring that they become autonomous Foundation Trusts.

We will make sure that funding decisions are made on the basis of need, and commissioning decisions according to evidence-based quality standards, by creating an independent NHS board to allocate resources and provide commissioning guidelines. We will ensure that NHS staff are protected if they raise concerns about patient safety.

NHS staff will be properly accountable to patients for their performance, removing the need for expensive layers of bureaucracy to oversee the NHS. As a result, we will be able to cut the cost of NHS administration by a third and transfer resources to support doctors and nurses on the frontline.

Increase access to vital drugs and services

People want an NHS that is easy to access at any time of day or night. We will commission a 24/7 urgent care service in every area of England, including GP out of hours services, and ensure that every patient can access a GP in their area between 8am and 8pm, seven days a week. We will introduce a single number for every kind of urgent care – to run in parallel with the emergency number 999.

We will stop the forced closure of A&E and maternity wards, so that people have better access to local services, and give mothers a real choice over where to have their baby, with NHS funding following their decisions. We will create local 'maternity networks' to ensure that mothers can safely access the right care, in the right place, at the right time.

When patients are forced to go to hospital, they expect the highest standards of cleanliness. But infections like MRSA now kill more than three times as many people as are killed on the roads each year. We will increase the number of single rooms in hospitals, as resources allow, helping the battle against infection and providing safety and privacy. As a result, we will end the scandal of mixed-sex accommodation – which Labour have failed to do. And we will not pay hospitals in full when a patient is left with an avoidable infection.

NHS patients rightly expect to be among the first in the world to access effective treatments, but under Labour they are among the last. We want more people to access the drugs and treatments that would prolong or improve their lives by reforming the way drug companies are paid for NHS medicines. Using money saved by the NHS through our pledge to stop Labour's jobs tax, we will create a Cancer Drug Fund to enable patients to access the cancer drugs their doctors think will help them.

To help the fight against cancer further, we will:

- give thousands more people – especially young people – access to effective drugs to treat rare cancers by changing the way these drugs are commissioned;

- encourage clinical trials of innovative techniques to diagnose and treat cancer; and,

- support the roll out of screening programmes for common cancers.

Under Labour, fewer people are able to see an NHS dentist. So we will introduce a new dentistry contract that will focus on achieving good dental health, not simply the number of treatments achieved. This will tie newly-qualified dentists into the NHS for five years and allow dentists to fine people who consistently miss appointments. These changes will allow us to give one million more people access to an NHS dentist and give every five year old a dental check-up.

Take control of your care

Where possible we want to devolve control over health budgets to the lowest possible level, so people have more control over their health needs. For people with a chronic illness or a long-term condition, we will provide access to a single budget that combines their health and social care funding, which they can tailor to their own needs.

The UK's six million carers play an indispensable role in looking after friends or family members who need support. Not only do they provide help to some of the most vulnerable people in society, the unpaid work they do contributes £87 billion worth of value a year – sometimes at the cost of carers' finances and even their health. We will support carers, and those they look after, by providing direct payments to help with care needs and by improving access to respite care.

We will provide £10 million a year beyond 2011 to support children's hospices in their vital work. And so that proper support for the most sick children and adults can continue in the setting of their choice, we will introduce a new per-patient funding system for all hospices and other providers of palliative care.

We reject Labour's plans for a compulsory 'death tax' on everyone to pay for social care, regardless of their needs. We want to create a system which is based on choice and which rewards the hundreds of thousands of people who care for an elderly relative full-time. So we will allow anyone to protect their home from being sold to fund residential care costs by paying a one-off insurance premium that is entirely voluntary. Independent experts suggest this should cost around £8,000. We will support older people to live independently at home and have access to the personal care they need. We will work to design a system where people can top up their premium – also voluntarily – to cover the costs of receiving care in their own home.

A healthier nation

Lifestyle-linked health problems like obesity and smoking, an ageing population, and the spread of infectious diseases are leading to soaring costs for the NHS. At the same time, the difference in male life expectancy between the richest and poorest areas in our country is now greater than during Victorian times.

We will turn the Department of Health into a Department for Public Health so that the promotion of good health and prevention of illness get the attention they need. We will provide separate public health funding to local communities, which will be accountable for – and paid according to – how successful they are in improving their residents' health. In addition, we will:

- introduce a health premium – weighting public
  health funding towards the poorest areas with
  the worst health outcomes;

- enable welfare-to-work providers and
  employers to purchase services from
  Mental Health Trusts; and,

- increase access to effective 'talking' therapies.

Sweden

Since the free schools programme was established in Sweden, over 1,000 new schools have opened. They have been founded by foundations, charities and others – and they have attracted pupils by offering better discipline and higher standards. Because any parent can take the money the Swedish Government spends on their child's education and choose the school they want, standards have risen across the board as every school does its best to satisfy parents.

Raise standards in schools

We will improve standards for all pupils and close the attainment gap between the richest and poorest. We will enhance the prestige and quality of the teaching profession, and give heads and teachers tough new powers of discipline. We will restore rigour to the curriculum and exam system and give every parent access to a good school.

Improving our school system is the most important thing we can do to make opportunity more equal and address our declining social mobility. But Britain is slipping down the world league tables in reading, Maths and Science, and violence in the classroom is a serious problem. We are falling behind other countries, and there is a growing gap between the richest and the poorest. We can't go on like this, for the sake of the next generations.

A Conservative government will give many more children access to the kind of education that is currently only available to the well-off: safe classrooms, talented and specialist teachers, access to the best curriculum and exams, and smaller schools with smaller class sizes with teachers who know the children's names.

Better teachers and tougher discipline

The single most important thing for a good education is for every child to have access to a good teacher. We will take steps to enhance the status of the teaching profession and ensure it attracts the best people. Schools – especially struggling ones – must be able to attract the best teachers and subject specialists, so we will give all head teachers the power to pay good teachers more.

We will expand Teach First and introduce two new programmes – Teach Now, for people looking to change career, and Troops to Teachers, for ex-service personnel – to get experienced, high-quality people into the profession.

We will make it easier for teachers to deal with violent incidents and remove disruptive pupils or items from the classroom. We believe heads are best placed to improve behaviour, which is why we will stop them being overruled by bureaucrats on exclusions.

To raise the status of teaching and toughen school discipline further, we will:

- raise the entry requirement for taxpayer-funded primary school teacher training;

- expect new graduates to have at least a 2:2 in their degree in order to qualify for state-funded training;

- pay the student loan repayments for top Maths and Science graduates for as long as they remain teachers, by redirecting some of the current teacher training budget;

- give teachers the strongest possible protection from false accusations; and,

- reinforce powers of discipline by strengthening home-school behaviour contracts.

A rigorous curriculum and exam system

Every child who is capable of reading should be doing so after two years in primary school. To make this happen, we will promote the teaching of systematic synthetic phonics and ensure that teachers are properly trained to teach using this method. To provide parents with the reassurance they need that their child is making progress, we will establish a simple reading test at the age of six.

We will reform the National Curriculum so that it is more challenging and based on evidence about what knowledge can be mastered by children at different ages. We will ensure that the primary curriculum is organised around subjects like Maths, Science and History. We will encourage setting so those who are struggling get extra help and the most able are stretched.

Under Labour, the exam system has become devalued. We will ensure that our exam system is measured against the most rigorous systems in the world. We will keep Key Stage 2 tests and league tables. We will reform them to make them more rigorous. We will make other exams more robust by giving universities and academics more say over their form and content. We want to develop proper vocational and technical education that engages young people and meets the needs of modern business. So we will establish Technical Academies across England, starting in at least twelve cities.

People expect to be able to make choices about the services they use, based on robust information about the quality on offer. So a Conservative government will reform school league tables so that schools can demonstrate they are stretching the most able and raising the attainment of the less able.

To improve school standards further, we will:

- allow all state schools the freedom to offer the same high quality international exams that private schools offer – including giving every pupil the chance to study separate sciences at GCSE;

- create 20,000 additional young apprenticeships;

- allow schools and colleges to offer workplace training;

- publish all performance data currently kept secret by the Department for Children, Schools and Families; and,

- establish a free online database of exam papers and marking schemes.

Give every parent access to a good school

Drawing on the experience of the Swedish school reforms and the charter school movement in the United States, we will break down barriers to entry so that any good education provider can set up a new Academy school. Our schools revolution will create a new generation of good small schools with smaller class sizes and high standards of discipline.

Our school reform programme is a major part of our anti-poverty strategy, which is why our first task will be to establish new Academy schools in the most deprived areas of the country. They will be beacons of excellence in areas where school standards are unacceptably low.

We want every child to benefit from our reforms. So all existing schools will have the chance to achieve Academy status, with 'outstanding' schools pre-approved, and we will extend the Academy programme to primary schools.

Education's real power lies in its ability to transform life chances, but we can't go on giving the poorest children the worst education. That is why we will introduce a pupil premium – extra funding for children from disadvantaged backgrounds.

The most vulnerable children deserve the very highest quality of care, so we will call a moratorium on the ideologically-driven closure of special schools. We will end the bias towards the inclusion of children with special needs in mainstream schools.

People have been far too ready to excuse failure in schools. We will ensure that the schools inspectorate Ofsted adopts a more rigorous and targeted inspection regime, reporting on performance only in the core areas related to teaching and learning. And any school that is in special measures for more than a year will be taken over immediately by a successful Academy provider. To give parents better access to a good school, we will:

- give parents the power to save local schools threatened by closure, allowing communities the chance to take over and run good small schools;

- make sure Academies have the freedoms that helped to make them so successful in the first place; and,

- ensure failing schools are inspected more often – with the best schools visited less frequently.

New York

New York shows that it is possible to get a grip and cut crime. Over the past twenty years, serious crime in New York has fallen by 80 per cent, thanks to proactive community-based policing and the intelligent use of new technologies and crime data.

Fight back against crime

We will fight back against the crime and anti-social behaviour that blights our communities. We will take steps to reduce the causes of crime, like poverty and broken families. We will put the criminal justice system on the side of responsible citizens, take tougher measures against knife criminals and crack down on the binge-drinking that leads to violence. We will cut paperwork to get police out on the street and give people democratic control over local policing. We will introduce honesty in sentencing and pay voluntary and private providers to reduce re-offending.

Recorded violent crime against the person has risen sharply under Labour, yet police officers spend more time on paperwork than they do out on patrol. Labour's obsession with bureaucratic targets and box-ticking is hindering the fight against crime. Their string of broken promises has undermined people's trust. We can't go on with the police filling in forms instead of fighting crime.

A Conservative government will help to mend our broken society – by cracking down on drink- and drug-fuelled violence, tackling re-offending, and intervening early to stop young people getting onto the conveyor belt to crime – in order to reduce the causes of crime and anti-social behaviour.

We will rebuild confidence in the criminal justice system so that people know it is on the side of victims and working for law-abiding people, not criminals. And we will reform the police, giving them back their professional discretion – getting them out of police stations and onto the street, fighting and preventing crime – in return for making them truly accountable to the people they serve.

Targeted measures to reduce the causes of crime

Under Labour's lax licensing regime, drink-fuelled violence and disorder are a blight on many communities. We will overhaul the Licensing Act to give local authorities and the police much stronger powers to remove licences from, or refuse to grant licences to, any premises that are causing problems. In addition, we will:

- allow councils and the police to shut down permanently any shop or bar found persistently selling alcohol to children;

- double the maximum fine for under-age alcohol sales to £20,000;

- raise taxes on those drinks linked to anti-social drinking, while abolishing Labour's new 'cider tax' on ordinary drinkers;

- ban off-licences and supermarkets from selling alcohol below cost price; and,

- permit local councils to charge more for late-night licences to pay for additional policing.

We recognise the need for criminal sanctions like ASBOs and fixed penalty notices, but they are blunt instruments that often fail their purpose of deterring people from committing more crime. We will introduce a series of early intervention measures, including grounding orders, to allow the police to use instant sanctions to deal with anti-social behaviour without criminalising young people unnecessarily.

Put the criminal justice system on the side of the public

Today, almost four out of every five people found guilty of a knife crime escape jail. We have to send a serious, unambiguous message that carrying a knife is totally unacceptable, so we will make it clear that anyone convicted of a knife crime can expect to face a prison sentence. We will introduce mobile knife scanners on streets and public transport, and extend the length of custodial sentences that can be awarded in a Magistrates' Court from six to twelve months.

Our criminal justice system often lets down the victims of crime, so we will ensure that victims and their families are better informed about the progress of criminal proceedings and release of offenders. So that the public can be confident their views are accounted for in deciding sentences, we will examine the case for greater Parliamentary scrutiny of sentencing guidelines. We will carry out a fundamental review of legal aid to make it work more efficiently, and examine ways of bringing in alternative sources of funding.

We will change the law so that anyone acting reasonably to stop a crime or apprehend a criminal is not arrested or prosecuted, and we will give householders greater legal protection if they have to defend themselves against intruders in their homes.

We will implement the Prisoners' Earnings Act 1996 to allow deductions from the earnings of prisoners in properly paid work to be paid into the Victims' Fund. We will use this Fund to deliver up to fifteen new rape crisis centres and give existing rape crisis centres stable, long-term funding. To help stop sexual violence before it occurs, we will ensure that the school curriculum includes teaching young people about sexual consent.

Reform the police

The police should be focusing on police work, not paperwork. A Conservative government will reduce the amount of paperwork that the police have to deal with, starting by scrapping the stop form entirely and reducing the burden of stop and search procedures. Any search will still be recorded but by an officer radioing in, rather than filling in paperwork. To allow the police to focus on fighting crime, we will:

- amend the health and safety laws that stand in the way of common sense policing;

- give police the power to identify offenders in order to protect the public and prevent crime;

- return charging discretion to the police for minor offences; and,

- process criminals more quickly by video-linking custody cells and courts.

Policing relies on consent. People want to know that the police are listening to them, and the police want to be able to focus on community priorities, not ticking boxes. We will replace the existing, invisible and unaccountable police authorities and make the police accountable to a directly-elected individual who will set policing priorities for local communities. They will be responsible for setting the budget and the strategy for local police forces, with the police retaining their operational independence.

Giving people democratic control over policing priorities is a huge step forward in the empowerment of local communities, and we will go further by giving people the information they need to challenge their neighbourhood police teams to cut crime.

We will oblige the police to publish detailed local crime data statistics every month, in an open and standardised format.

Extremists, serious criminals and others find our borders far too easy to penetrate. That is why we will create a dedicated Border Police Force, as part of a refocused Serious Organised Crime Agency, to enhance national security, improve immigration controls, and crack down on the trafficking of people, weapons and drugs. We will work with police forces to strengthen arrangements to deal with serious crime and other cross-boundary policing challenges, and extend collaboration between forces to deliver better value for money.

Prisons with a purpose

In the last three years, 80,000 criminals have been released early from prison because the Government failed to build enough places. We are determined that early release will not be introduced again, so we will redevelop the prison estate and increase capacity as necessary to stop it. Under Labour, the number of foreign criminals in our prisons has more than doubled. We will extend early deportation of foreign national prisoners to reduce further the pressure on our prison population.

Many people feel that sentencing in Britain is dishonest and misleading. So we will introduce a system where the courts can specify minimum and maximum sentences for certain offenders. These prisoners will only be able to leave jail after their minimum sentence is served by having earned their release, not simply by right.

At the moment, many prisoners leave jail and lapse back into a life of drink, drugs and re-offending. We will never bring our crime rate down or start to reduce the costs of crime until we properly rehabilitate ex-prisoners. So, with a Conservative government, when offenders leave prison, they will be trained and rehabilitated by private and voluntary sector providers, under supervision. We will use the same approach that lies behind our welfare reform plans – payment by results – to cut re-offending, with organisations paid using savings made in the criminal justice system from the resulting lower levels of crime.

Drug and alcohol addiction are behind many of the crimes that are committed on our streets, but the treatment that too many addicts receive just maintains their habits. We will give courts the power to use abstinence-based Drug Rehabilitation Orders to help offenders kick drugs once and for all. We will introduce a system of temporary bans on new 'legal highs' while health issues are considered by independent experts.

To reform our system of rehabilitation further, we will:

- apply our payment by results reforms to the youth justice system;

- engage with specialist organisations to provide education, mentoring and drug rehabilitation programmes to help young offenders go straight; and,

- pilot a scheme to create Prison and Rehabilitation Trusts so that just one organisation is responsible for helping to stop a criminal re-offending.

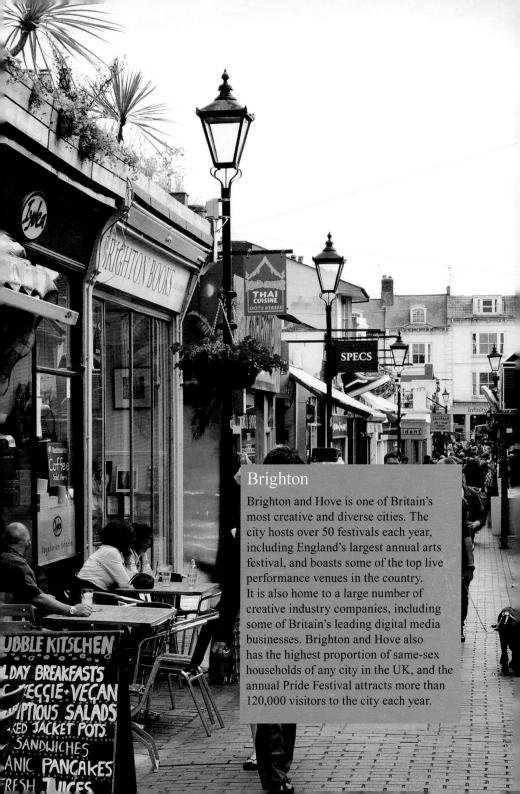

Brighton

Brighton and Hove is one of Britain's most creative and diverse cities. The city hosts over 50 festivals each year, including England's largest annual arts festival, and boasts some of the top live performance venues in the country. It is also home to a large number of creative industry companies, including some of Britain's leading digital media businesses. Brighton and Hove also has the highest proportion of same-sex households of any city in the UK, and the annual Pride Festival attracts more than 120,000 visitors to the city each year.

Change politics

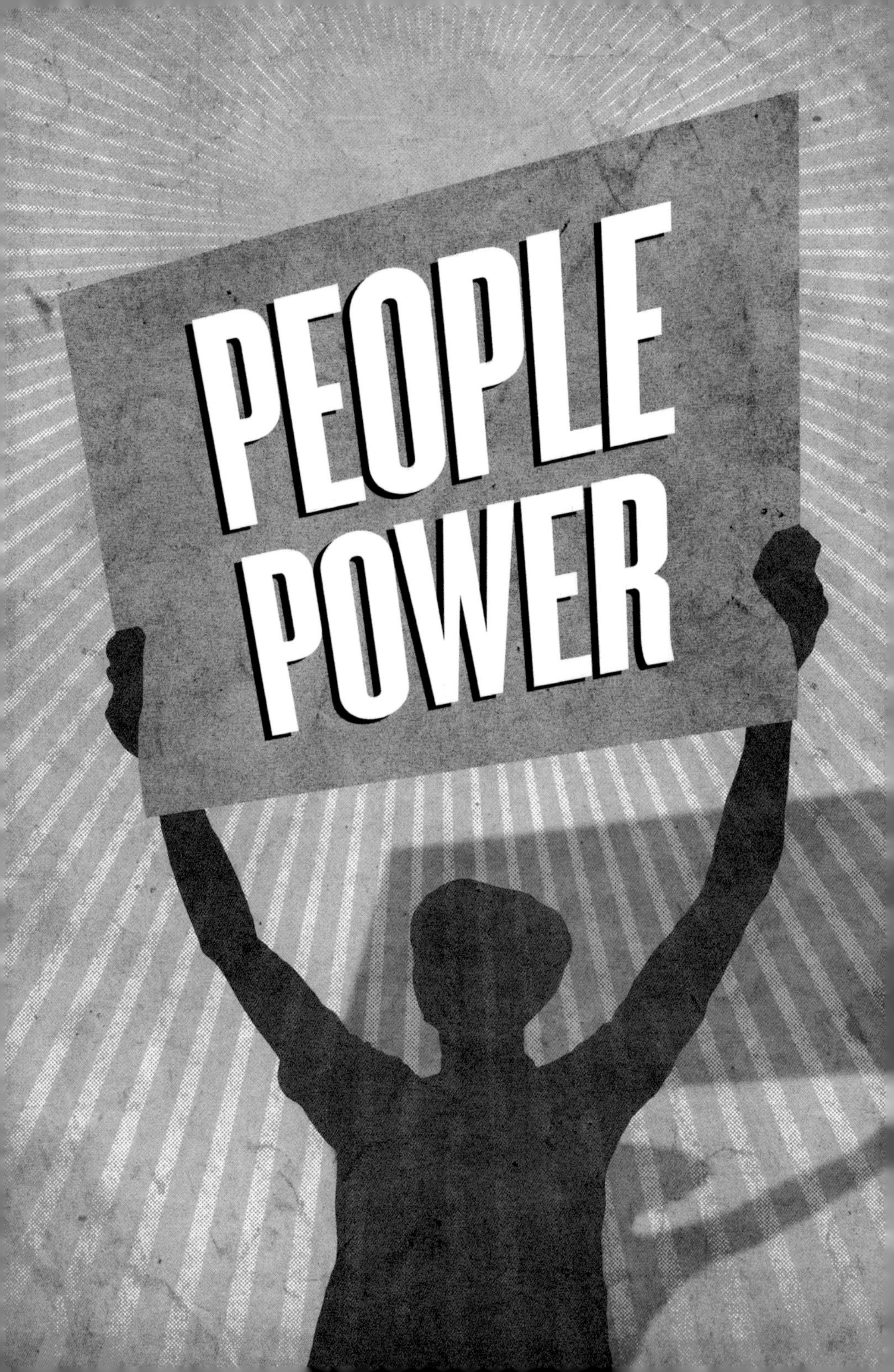
PEOPLE
POWER

A new agenda for a new politics

The Conservative Party has led the way in sorting out the mess of MPs' expenses. In government we will go further, by cutting the size of Parliament, cutting the scope of Whitehall, and cutting the cost of politics. We will make politics more local, more transparent and more accountable. We intend to build a new political system that serves people rather than politicians. Together, we can change our politics for the better.

The events of recent months have revealed the size of the fissures in our political system. Millions of people in this country are at best detached from democracy, at worst angry and disillusioned. This endangers our ability to work together to solve our common problems. Just putting this down to the shocking revelations of the expenses scandal would be a great mistake. MPs' expenses might have been the trigger for the public's anger, but this political crisis is driven by a deeper sense of frustration – that people have too little control over the decisions that affect their daily lives.

The top-down model of power that exists in Britain today is completely out of date. The argument that has applied for well over a century – that in every area of life we need people at the centre to make sense of the world for us and take decisions on our behalf – has collapsed. We now live in an age when technology can put information that was previously held by a few into the hands of the many. This is an age of personal freedom and choice, when culture and debate are shaped by a multitude of voices. But politics has not caught up with this new age. Instead of giving people more power over their lives, we have a government intent on taking it away.

We believe in people power – and today the information revolution gives us the practical tools to realise that philosophy. So we plan to change Britain with a sweeping redistribution of power: from the state to citizens; from the government to Parliament; from Whitehall to communities; from Brussels to Britain; from bureaucracy to democracy. Taking power away from the political elite and handing it to the man and woman in the street. Using decentralisation, accountability and transparency, we will weaken the old political elites, give people power, fix our broken politics and restore people's faith that if we act together things can change. This is a new agenda for a new politics.

Shaun Bailey

"We need a new kind of politics in this country, a politics where people join because they want to do something, not because they want to be someone. We need to reverse the relationship between politicians and people so that it's the people demanding respect from politicians, not the other way around. I've spent my career working with and for the people of my community, and now I'm hoping to be fighting for that community in Parliament. This manifesto is a call to action for all of us to take control and do our bit in our communities."

Shaun Bailey is a youth worker and is the Conservative candidate for Hammersmith and Shepherd's Bush

Make politics more accountable

We will clean up politics: the expenses, the lobbying and problems with party funding. We will cut the cost of Parliament, cut the number of MPs and cut Ministers' pay. We will give citizens direct control over what goes on in Westminster, make government more accountable and safeguard the independence of the civil service.

It is vital that we act quickly and decisively to restore the reputation of politics. Too much unacceptable behaviour has gone unchecked for too long, from excessive expenses to sleazy lobbying practices. The people of Britain have looked on in horror as revelations have stripped away the dignity of Parliament, leaving millions of voters detached from the political process, devoid of trust in the political classes, and disillusioned with our system of government.

We will act rapidly to push through far-reaching reforms to restore ethics to politics and revive the electorate's faith in politicians. It will take nothing less than a deep clean of the political system in Westminster to root out the sleaze and dispel suspicion. We will start by cleaning up the expenses system to ensure MPs live by the same standards as the people who give them their jobs, and by curbing the way in which former Ministers have secured lobbying jobs by exploiting their contacts.

But that is just the start. We will also cut Ministers' pay and reduce the number of MPs in Parliament. Then we will go further,

far further, since the expenses scandal was just the trigger for a deeper sense of frustration. We promise a total overhaul of our system of government, so that power is passed from the politicians at Westminster back to the people of Britain. But this is the very least that is needed to fix our broken political system.

Clean up Westminster

The political crisis was triggered by the scandal of MPs' expenses. We were the Party that insisted that MPs' expenses were published online, and we have supported the independent proposals to clean up the House of Commons. We proposed legislation so that anyone wanting to be a member of either the House of Commons or the House of Lords will need to be treated as a full UK taxpayer. But much, much more is needed to clean up our politics and restore public trust.

At the moment, there is no way that local constituents can remove an MP found guilty of serious wrongdoing until there is a general election. That is why a Conservative government will introduce a power of 'recall' to allow electors to kick out MPs, a power that will be triggered by proven serious wrongdoing. And we will introduce a Parliamentary Privilege Act to make clear that privilege cannot be abused by MPs to evade justice.

The cost of politics has spiralled out of control. We will cut the perks and bureaucracy associated with Parliament to save over £100 million a year. We will consult with the Independent Parliamentary Standards Authority on how to move away from the generous final-salary pension system for MPs.

The public are concerned about the influence of money on politics, whether it is from trade unions, individuals, or the lobbying industry. We will seek an agreement on a comprehensive package of reform that will encourage individual donations and include an across-the-board cap on donations. This will mark the end of the big donor era and the problems it has sometimes entailed.

A Conservative government will introduce new measures to ensure that the contacts and knowledge Ministers gain while being paid by the public to serve the public are not unfairly used for private gain. We will:

- ensure that ex-Ministers are banned from lobbying government for two years after leaving office;

- ensure that ex-Ministers have to seek advice on the business posts they take up for ten years after leaving office;

- rewrite the Ministerial Code to make clear that any former Minister who breaks the rules on appointments will be forced to give up some or all of their Ministerial pension; and,

- introduce new rules to stop central government bodies using public money to hire lobbyists to lobby other government bodies.

The lobbying industry must regulate itself to ensure its practices are transparent – if it does not, then we will legislate to do so.

Give citizens more power

People have been shut out of Westminster politics for too long. Having a single vote every four or five years is not good enough – we need to give people real control over how they are governed. So, with a Conservative government, any petition that secures 100,000 signatures will be eligible for formal debate in Parliament. The petition with the most signatures will enable members of the public to table a Bill eligible to be voted on in Parliament. And we will introduce a new Public Reading Stage for Bills to give the public an opportunity to comment on proposed legislation online.

Labour have meddled shamelessly with the electoral system to try to gain political advantage. A Conservative government will ensure every vote will have equal value by introducing 'fair vote' reforms to equalise the size of constituency electorates, and conduct a boundary review to implement these changes within five years. We will swiftly implement individual voter registration, giving everyone the right to cast their vote in person and making it easier for UK citizens living overseas to vote.

We support the first-past-the-post system for Westminster elections because it gives voters the chance to kick out a government they are fed up with. We will work to build a consensus for a mainly-elected second chamber to replace the current House of Lords, recognising that an efficient and effective second chamber should play an important role in our democracy and requires both legitimacy and public confidence.

Make government more accountable and representative

Because we are serious about redistributing power, we will restore the balance between the government and Parliament, by:

- establishing a Backbench Business Committee to give the House of Commons more control over its own timetable;

- allowing MPs the time to scrutinise law effectively;

- providing more free votes, and protecting the principle that issues of conscience – like abortion – remain subject to a free vote; and,

- making the use of the Royal Prerogative subject to greater democratic control so that Parliament is properly involved in all big national decisions.

We will scrap Labour's failed target regime and instead require every department to publish a business plan, with senior management accountable to more rigorous departmental boards for their performance. We will make it easier to reward the best civil servants and remove the least effective. We will reform the Civil Service Compensation Scheme to bring it more into line with practice in the private sector. We will put a limit on the number of special advisers and protect the impartiality of the civil service.

Rebuilding trust in politics means making our political system better reflect the people it is meant to represent. We will introduce a £1 million fund to help people with disabilities who want to become MPs, councillors or other elected officials with the extra costs they face in running for office. This will be funded from the existing budget of the Government Equalities Office.

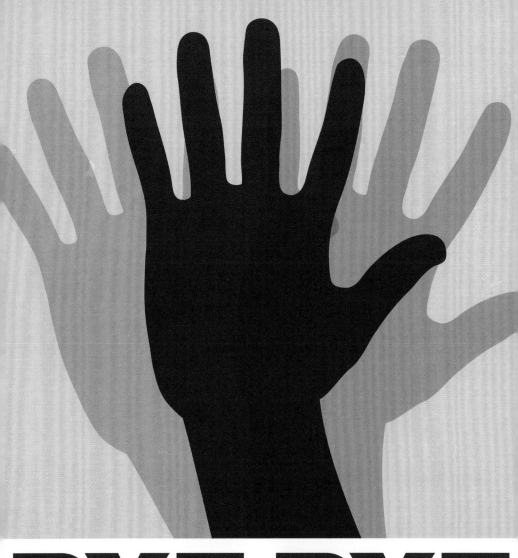

BYE BYE
BUREAUCRACY

Make politics more transparent

We will publish details of the money government spends and the people it employs. People will have a right to government data to make the performance of the state transparent. We will cut the unaccountable quango state and root out waste.

Government has been far too profligate for far too long. Billions are wasted each year on pointless bureaucracy and failed projects while taxpayers are left to foot the bill. The explosion of unaccountable quangos, public sector 'non-jobs' and costly bureaucracy is an indictment of Labour's reckless approach to spending other people's money. Once again, it undermines public trust in the political process.

We understand that people want government to be more effective in what it does, and to do it for less money. That means transforming the way the state goes about its business, using decentralisation, accountability and transparency to reduce dramatically the cost of government. And, because sunlight is the best disinfectant, we will bring the operation of government out into the open so that everyone can see whether we are delivering good value for money.

Publish data so the public can hold government to account

Drawing inspiration from administrations around the world which have shown that being transparent can transform the effectiveness of government, we will create a powerful new right to government data, enabling the public to request – and receive – government datasets in an open and standardised format. Independent estimates suggest this could provide a £6 billion boost to the UK economy. We will open up Whitehall recruitment by publishing central government job vacancies online, saving costs and increasing transparency.

A Conservative government will bring in new measures to enable the public to scrutinise the government's accounts to see whether it is providing value for money. All data will be published in an open and standardised format. We will:

- require public bodies to publish online the job titles of every member of staff and the salaries and expenses of senior officials paid more than the lowest salary permissible in Pay Band 1 of the Senior Civil Service pay scale, and organograms that include all positions in those bodies;

- require anyone paid more than the Prime Minister in the public sector to have their salary signed off by the Treasury;

- require senior civil servants to publish online details of expense claims and meetings with lobbyists;

- apply these transparency principles to local government, with the threshold for publication of spending items and contracts set at £500, and for the publication of salaries the same as at the national level; and,

- give councillors the power to vote on large salary packages for unelected council officials.

Curtail the quango state

Under Labour, the quango state has flourished. Government figures show that there are over 700 unelected bodies spending £46 billion every year, but this does not even include the range of advisory bodies, public corporations, taskforces and regional government bodies that have sprung up under Labour. We believe that Ministers should be responsible for government policy, not unelected bureaucrats. Any quangos that do not perform a technical function or a function that requires political impartiality, or act independently to establish facts, will be abolished. To increase the scrutiny of quangos, we will:

- give Select Committees the right to hold confirmation hearings for major public appointments, including the heads of quangos;

- examine the case for giving Select Committees the power to prevent increases in quango budgets; and,

- ensure that the National Audit Office has full access to the BBC's accounts.

Reduce the cost of procurement

This government has a dreadful record of managing procurement, with billions of pounds wasted on mismanaged projects. We will tackle wasteful government procurement projects by:

- strengthening the role of the Chief Information Officer to get a grip on government ICT projects;

- introducing a series of changes to ICT procurement to deliver better value for money;

- appointing senior private sector non-executives to departmental boards to deliver better value for money;

- publishing in full government contracts for goods and services worth over £25,000; and,

- increasing the accountability of EU spending by publishing details of every UK project that receives over £25,000 of EU funds.

Average population, lowest tier of executive government

France   1,750

Austria   3,540

Spain   5,620

Germany   6,655

Italy   7,395

Netherlands 37,280

UK   151,110

Source: Council of European Municipalities and Regions and Dexia, 2008

Make politics more local

We will put neighbourhoods in charge of planning the way their communities develop, with incentives in favour of sustainable development. We will make it easier for everyone to get onto the housing ladder. We will give individuals and local government much more power, allow communities to take control of vital services, and give people the chance to have a powerful, elected mayor in England's largest cities.

Over the last forty years, governments of all colours have been guilty of weakening local government. But what was a gradual centralisation has accelerated dramatically under Labour. Bureaucratic control has replaced democratic accountability. The wishes of local people are second-guessed by bureaucrats; the activities of councils are micro-managed by unelected quangos. This hoarding of power by distant politicians and unaccountable officials in Whitehall has damaged society by eroding trust.

We believe that the more responsibility you give people, the more responsibly they behave. That is why we are so determined to give people much more power and control over their lives. Citizens themselves should have a direct say over how they are governed – but not through bureaucratic consultations or phoney citizens juries, which never change anything. We need a totally different approach to governing, one that involves people in making the decisions that affect them. This is what we call collaborative democracy – people

taking the kind of powers that until now have been exercised only by governments. So we want to pass power down to people – to individuals where we can. But it is not always possible to give power to individuals, and in those cases we need to push power down to the most appropriate local level: neighbourhood, community and local government.

Put communities in charge of planning

The planning system is vital for a strong economy, for an attractive and sustainable environment, and for a successful democracy. A Conservative government will introduce a new 'open source' planning system. This will mean that people in each neighbourhood will be able to specify what kind of development they want to see in their area. These neighbourhood plans will be consolidated into a local plan.

We will abolish the entire bureaucratic and undemocratic tier of regional planning, including the Regional Spatial Strategies and building targets.

Developers will have to pay a tariff to the local authority to compensate the community for loss of amenity and costs of additional infrastructure. The tariff will replace the payments and levies on development that have grown up under Labour. A portion of this tariff will be kept by the neighbourhoods in which a given development takes place, providing clear incentives for communities which go for growth.

Significant local projects, like new housing estates, will have to be designed through a collaborative process that has involved the neighbourhood. Immediate neighbours will have a new role – with a faster approvals process for planning applications where neighbours raise no objections.

At the national level, for all forms of development, we will publish and present to Parliament for debate a simple and consolidated national planning framework, which will set out national economic and environmental priorities.

To give communities greater control over planning, we will:

- abolish the power of planning inspectors to rewrite local plans;

- amend the 'Use Classes Order' so that people can use buildings for any purpose allowed in the local plan;

- limit appeals against local planning decisions to cases that involve abuse of process or failure to apply the local plan;

- encourage county councils and unitary authorities to compile infrastructure plans;

- give local planning authorities and other public authorities a duty to co-operate with one another; and,

- allow neighbourhoods to stop the practice of 'garden grabbing'.

Deliver more affordable homes

We want to create a property-owning democracy where everyone has the chance to own their own home. That is why we will permanently raise the stamp duty threshold to £250,000 for first-time buyers, meaning nine out of ten of them will pay no tax on their first home purchase.

Communities should benefit when they choose to develop sustainably, so we will match pound-for-pound the council tax receipts that local authorities receive from new homes to encourage sensitive local development. We will create new local housing trusts to allow communities to grant planning permission for new housing within villages and towns

– so that the benefits of development remain within the local area. We will also abolish Home Information Packs, which have made a significant contribution to problems in our housing market.

A Conservative government will make it easier for social tenants to own or part-own their home. We will:

- introduce a 'foot on the ladder' programme to offer an equity stake to good social tenants, which can be cashed in when they move out of social rented accommodation;

- pilot a new 'right to move' scheme and introduce a nationwide social home swap programme, so social tenants can transfer their tenancy to another home or part of the country; and,

- respect the tenures and rents of social housing tenants.

We will implement a range of measures to address the problems of the homeless, including introducing more accurate street counts and ensuring a Minister in each relevant department has homelessness in their brief.

Give people more power and control over their lives

We have set out our plans to give more power to people over the way they are policed, the schools their children go to and the hospitals they are treated in. But, in addition, we want to give individuals more direct control over how they are governed. So, mirroring our reforms at the national level, we will give residents the power to instigate local referendums on any local issue if 5 per cent of the local population sign up, and they will also be able to veto any proposed high council tax increases. We will stop Labour's plans to impose supplementary business rates on firms if a majority do not give their consent.

Nothing underlines the powerlessness that many communities feel more than the loss of essential services, like post offices and pubs, because of decisions made by distant bureaucrats. Our new 'community right to buy' scheme will give local people the power to protect any community assets that are threatened with closure. In addition, we will:

- give people a 'right to bid' to run any community service instead of the state; and,

- reform the governance arrangements in football to enable co-operative ownership models to be established by supporters.

We will give democratically accountable local government much greater power to improve their citizens' lives by:

- giving local councils a 'general power of competence', so that they have explicit authority to do what is necessary to improve their communities;

- ending ring-fencing so that funding can be spent on local priorities;

- scrapping the hundreds of process targets Labour have imposed on councils;

- ending the bureaucratic inspection regime that stops councils focusing on residents' main concerns;

- scrapping Labour's uncompleted plans to impose unwieldy and expensive unitary councils and to force the regionalisation of the fire service;

- ending the 'predetermination rules' that prevent councillors speaking up about issues that they have campaigned on; and,

- encouraging the greater use of ward budgets for councillors.

We have seen that a single municipal leader can inject dynamism and ambition into their communities. So, initially, we will give the citizens in each of England's twelve largest cities the chance of having an elected mayor. Big decisions should be made by those who are democratically accountable, not by remote and costly quangos. We will abolish the Government Office for London as part of our plan to devolve more power downwards to the London Boroughs and the Mayor of London.

Decentralising control must go hand in hand with creating much greater transparency in local government. Power without information is not enough. We will implement fully the Sustainable Communities Act, and reintroduce the Sustainable Communities Act (Amendment) Bill as government legislation, to give people greater information on, and control over, what is being spent by each government agency in their area.

Our plans to decentralise power will only work properly if there is a strong, independent and vibrant local media to hold local authorities to account. We will sweep away the rules that stop local newspapers owning other local media platforms and create a new network of local television stations. And we will tighten the rules on taxpayer-funded publicity spending by town halls.

Current powers of entry, average introduced per year

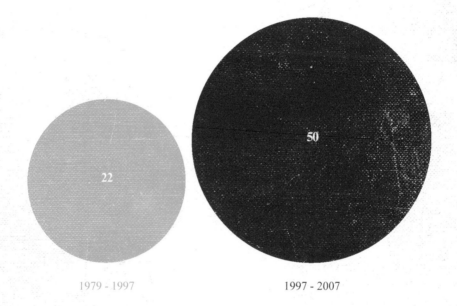

22

1979 - 1997

50

1997 - 2007

Source: Home Office

Restore our civil liberties

We will scale back Labour's database state and protect the privacy of the public's information. We will introduce a balanced approach to the retention of people's DNA and reform the criminal records system so it protects children without destroying trust.

Labour have subjected Britain's historic freedoms to unprecedented attack. They have trampled on liberties and, in their place, compiled huge databases to track the activities of millions of perfectly innocent people, giving public bodies extraordinary powers to intervene in the way we live our lives.

The impact of this has been profound and far-reaching. Trust has been replaced by suspicion. The database state is a poor substitute for the human judgement essential to the delivery of public services. Worse than that, it gives people false comfort that an infallible central state is looking after their best interests. But the many scandals of lost data, leaked documents and database failures have put millions at risk. It is time for a new approach to protecting our liberty.

Protect our freedoms

Labour's approach to our personal privacy is the worst of all worlds – intrusive, ineffective and enormously expensive. We will scrap ID cards, the National Identity Register and the Contactpoint database. To protect our freedoms from state encroachment and encourage greater social responsibility, we will replace the Human Rights Act with a UK Bill of Rights. We will review and reform libel laws to protect freedom of speech, reduce costs and discourage libel tourism.

Wherever possible, we believe that personal data should be controlled by individual citizens themselves. We will strengthen the powers of the Information Commissioner to penalise any public body found guilty of mismanaging data. We will take further steps to protect people from unwarranted intrusion by the state, including:

- cutting back intrusive powers of entry into homes, which have been massively extended under Labour;

- curtailing the surveillance powers that allow some councils to use anti-terrorism laws to spy on people making trivial mistakes or minor breaches of the rules;

- requiring Privacy Impact Assessments of any proposal that involves data collection or sharing; and,

- ensuring proper Parliamentary scrutiny of any new powers of data-sharing.

The indefinite retention of innocent people's
DNA is unacceptable, yet DNA data provides
a useful tool for solving crimes. We will legislate
to make sure that our DNA database is used
primarily to store information about those who
are guilty of committing crimes rather than
those who are innocent. We will collect the
DNA of all existing prisoners, those under
state supervision who have been convicted of
an offence, and anyone convicted of a serious
recordable offence. We pushed the Government
to end the permanent retention of innocent
people's DNA, and we will change the guidance
to give people on the database who have been
wrongly accused of a minor crime an automatic
right to have their DNA withdrawn.

We believe that people working in positions
of trust with children should go through a
proper criminal record check. But Labour's
new system goes too far. So we will review
the criminal records and 'vetting and barring'
regime and scale it back to common sense levels.

The Hunting Act has proved unworkable.
A Conservative government will give Parliament
the opportunity to repeal the Hunting Act
on a free vote, with a government bill in
government time.

Strengthen the Union

We are a unionist party and we will not put the Union at risk. But we support devolution and are committed to making it work for all countries. We will take forward the proposals of the Calman Commission, grant a referendum on greater powers for the Welsh Assembly, and support the devolved institutions in Northern Ireland. We will rebalance the unfairness in the voting system for devolved issues in Parliament.

In recent years, we have been hearing things that we have not heard for a long time: people in Scotland saying they want to leave the UK, and some people responding with 'let them go'. Labour's constitutional vandalism has weakened Parliament, undermined democracy and brought the integrity of the ballot into question. Our unbalanced devolution settlement has caused separatism to gather momentum in Scotland, and separatists have propped up a weakened Labour Party in Wales.

The Conservative Party is passionate about the Union and we will never do anything to put it at risk. And, because of the new political force we have created with the Ulster Unionists, we are proud that at the next election we will be the only party fielding candidates in every part of the UK.

Support devolution

We support the changes proposed by the Calman Commission for clarifying the devolution settlement and creating a relationship of mutual respect between Westminster and Holyrood:

- The Prime Minister and other Ministers will go to Holyrood for questioning on a regular basis.

- The Scottish Parliament should have more responsibility for raising the money it spends. We will produce our own White Paper by May 2011 to set out how we will deal with the issues raised by Calman, and we will legislate to implement those proposals within the next Parliament.

We will not stand in the way of the referendum on further legislative powers requested by the Welsh Assembly. The people of Wales will decide the outcome and Conservatives will have a free vote. But our priority remains getting people back into work and strengthening the Welsh economy. So we will seek ways to work with the Welsh Assembly Government to increase economic growth and improve people's quality of life.

In Northern Ireland, we strongly support the political institutions established over the past decade and we are committed to making devolution work. We will continue to promote peace, stability and economic prosperity and work to bring Northern Ireland back into the mainstream of UK politics. We will produce a government paper examining the mechanism for changing the corporation tax rate in Northern Ireland, in order to attract significant new investment. And we will stop the practice of 'double-jobbing', whereby elected representatives sit in both Westminster and Stormont.

Labour have refused to address the so-called 'West Lothian Question': the unfair situation of Scottish MPs voting on matters which are devolved. A Conservative government will introduce new rules so that legislation referring specifically to England, or to England and Wales, cannot be enacted without the consent of MPs representing constituencies of those countries.

Strangford Lough, County Down

Farming is at the heart of the rural economy, and a significant cultural influence in British life. Over half a million people are employed in the farming industry, which makes use of three quarters of the UK's land area and generates over £4 billion of economic income for the UK each year. Organic farming has become increasingly important in recent years, with over 5,000 organic farms now occupying 700,000 hectares of land. In Northern Ireland, farming's share of employment and economic activity is larger than in any other part of the UK.

Protect the environment

Vote blue, go green

A Conservative government will cut carbon emissions and rebuild our energy security. We will make it easier for people to go green, with incentives for people to do the right thing. We will protect our precious habitats and natural resources, and promote a sustainable farming industry. We will fulfil our responsibility to hand on a richer and more sustainable natural environment to future generations.

We have a vision of a greener Britain. It is a country that leads the world in the market for green goods and services. A new hi-tech manufacturing sector and a new Green Investment Bank help create new jobs, wealth and growth. Our cars run on electricity and high speed trains take us across the country in less time than it takes to get across the capital. This is a country which has become the world's first low carbon economy.

In this vision, our homes require less energy and more of the energy we produce comes from renewable sources. Our countryside is better cared for, we conserve more natural habitats, and we create new green spaces and plant many more trees. Our landscape is protected and our wildlife is enjoyed by more people of all ages. It is a greener and more pleasant land for all its citizens.

This is a Conservative vision for our future, and it is based on Conservative values. We believe that it is our responsibility to create a clean and healthy environment to pass on to our children. That is why we have put green issues back at the heart of our politics and that is why they will be at the heart of our government.

Instead of using rules and regulations to impose a centralised worldview, we will go with the grain of human nature, creating new incentives and market signals which reward people for doing the right thing. Instead of pulling bureaucratic levers from above telling people what they can't do, we will provide people with the information they need to make more responsible choices. Instead of holding businesses back by imposing unfair retrospective stealth taxes, we will unleash the power of green enterprise and promote resource efficiency to generate thousands of green jobs. This is how we will live up to our responsibility to be the greenest government in our history.

Freiburg

Freiburg in Germany is a world leader in environmental sustainability. Solar panels have been installed across the city – on schools, churches and private houses, and even on the sports stadium and the City Hall. Over the past 30 years, 500km of bike lanes and 9,000 bike parking sites have been put in place and, as a result, Freiburg now has the lowest car usage of any city in Germany. Freiburg also has one of the highest recycling rates of any city in the world, which has been achieved by changing social norms and providing facilities that make it as easy as possible for people to recycle. This emphasis on sustainability has had an economic benefit too: Freiburg is home to 1,500 green technology companies, which employ over 10,000 people and generate hundreds of millions of euros for the local economy.

Combat climate change

We will reduce carbon emissions in line with our international commitments. We will promote small- and large-scale low carbon energy production, including nuclear, wind, clean coal and biogas. We will safeguard our energy security by ensuring there is sufficient spare capacity in the energy system. We will make it easier to go green, including through a 'Green Deal' to cut household energy bills.

Labour's failure on climate change has been stark. Strong rhetoric has not been matched by effective action – it took the longest and deepest recession for sixty years for Labour to achieve any significant reduction in the UK's carbon emissions. We need to generate 15 per cent of our energy from renewables by 2020, but we have one of the worst records of any EU nation when it comes to renewable energy. Our national security is threatened by a looming energy crunch in which a third of our electricity generating capacity will close, and most of our gas will need to be imported by 2020.

Yet Britain is uniquely placed to be the world's first low carbon economy: we have the natural resources to generate wind and wave power, a skilled workforce trained in the energy industry, a hi-tech manufacturing sector and a green financial centre in the City of London. We urgently need to make this transition in order to strengthen our economy, help guarantee our energy security and protect our environment for future generations.

Ambitious goals for reducing emissions

Climate change is a global phenomenon, and that means the world must work together to reduce harmful emissions. A Conservative government will work towards an ambitious global deal that will limit emissions and make available substantial financial resources for adaptation and mitigation.

As part of our commitment to move towards a low carbon future, we can confirm our aim of reducing carbon emissions by 80 per cent by 2050. In government, we will lead from the front by delivering a 10 per cent cut in central government emissions within twelve months and by working with local authorities and others to deliver emissions reductions.

Promote low carbon energy production

The way our energy is produced and transmitted is stuck in the last century. A Conservative government will transform this 'dumb', unresponsive network and create an 'electricity internet' – a highly interactive network, based on a new smart grid that will interact with smart meters in people's homes, to manage supply and demand. This will allow a huge increase in renewable power, and far greater choice for consumers.

To limit harmful emissions from UK power stations, we will take steps to encourage new low carbon energy production, including:

- introducing an Emissions Performance Standard to limit the levels of greenhouse gases our power stations produce;

- clearing the way for new nuclear power stations – provided they receive no public subsidy;

- creating four carbon capture and storage-equipped plants, taking coal – one of the most polluting fuels of all – and transforming it into a low carbon fuel of the future;

- delivering an offshore electricity grid in order to support the development of a new generation of offshore wind power, and establishing at least two Marine Energy Parks;

- giving local authorities the power to establish new district heating networks which use biogas and other low carbon fuels;

- allowing communities that host renewable energy projects like wind farms to keep the additional business rates they generate for six years; and,

- giving incentives for smaller-scale energy generation, including capturing heat that is currently wasted.

Safeguard the UK's energy security

Britain has had no clear energy policy for thirteen years. A succession of eleven energy Ministers and eight Secretaries of State with responsibility for energy has left our policy muddled and put our energy security at risk. Britain needs an energy policy that is clear, consistent and stable. That means that Ministers will be unambiguously responsible for determining energy policy and delivering an Annual Energy Statement to Parliament to set a clear direction for energy policy. To safeguard our energy security, we will reform the energy regulator Ofgem so that:

- it focuses on executing energy policy;

- it is tasked with monitoring the spare capacity in the energy market and making provisions for additional capacity where required; and,

- its competition policy and consumer protection powers pass to the Office of Fair Trading.

As a result, we will cut the number of quangos intervening in the energy market.

Labour's just-in-time approach to energy supply has left us badly exposed to events outside our control. We will work to diversify the sources of the gas we need, secure long-term contracts and increase storage capacity to guarantee supplies throughout the year.

Help people go green

Rising energy costs hit families hard, so we will create a 'Green Deal', giving every home up to £6,500 worth of energy improvement measures – with more for hard-to-treat homes – paid for out of savings made on fuel bills over 25 years.

We will increase consumers' control over their energy costs by ensuring that every energy bill provides information on how to move to the cheapest tariff offered by their supplier and how their energy usage compares to similar households.

We will improve the energy efficiency of everyday appliances by drawing on the experience of the 'top runner' scheme from Japan.

To help further, we will:

- ensure that 10 per cent of the staff directly employed by 'Green Deal' providers are apprentices, helping to build a green collar workforce for the future;

- keep Energy Performance Certificates to help people improve the environmental rating of their property; and,

- give Post Office Card Account holders the chance to benefit from direct debit discounts, worth up to £150 a year.

Recycling rates

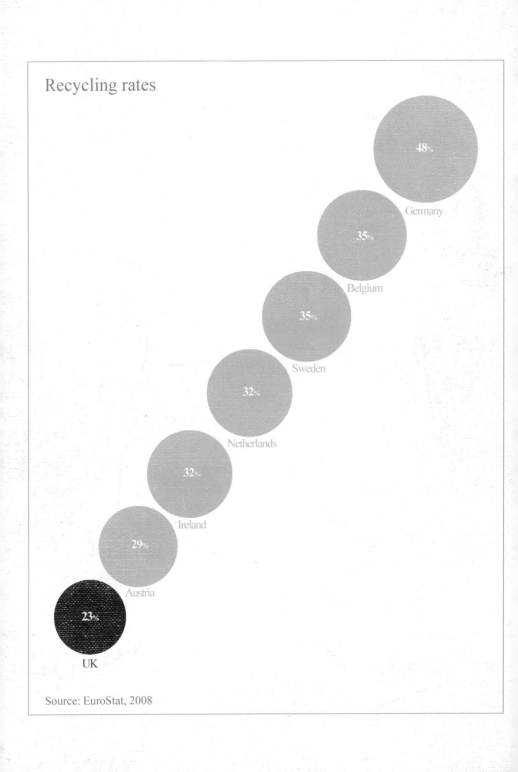

48% Germany

35% Belgium

35% Sweden

32% Netherlands

32% Ireland

29% Austria

23% UK

Source: EuroStat, 2008

Conserve and enhance the natural environment

We will protect and improve the UK's natural environment, and pioneer new schemes to improve conservation. We will push for reform of the Common Agricultural and Fisheries Policies to promote sustainable farming and fishing. We will promote high animal welfare standards and ensure that government procures locally-produced food wherever possible. We will work towards a zero-waste society.

Conservatives understand the inherent value of conserving things, and we know the importance of ensuring that we provide a good quality of life for future generations. Our natural environment has been degraded and urgent action is needed to address the loss of vital ecosystems in the face of climate change and development. Labour have relied too much on regulation and top-down targets that have failed to halt biodiversity loss.

We need to act now to enhance biodiversity, protect our countryside and marine environment, and secure the vital eco-systems that sustain life on land, in our rivers and in our seas. A Conservative government will take a broad approach to improving the natural environment as a whole, so that we can ensure a secure future for the natural world where vital ecological assets are protected and resources are used more responsibly.

Conserve wildlife

Too many animals remain at risk of extinction, and climate change will put even more pressure on endangered species and precious habitats.

We will support the strongest protection for endangered species and work to protect vital habitats from destruction. We will tackle the smuggling and illegal trade in wildlife through our new Border Police Force.

We will fight for wholesale reform of the Common Fisheries Policy to encourage sustainable practices, give communities a greater say over the future of their fishing industries, and bring an end to the scandal of fish discards. We will take forward the Marine and Coastal Access Act and ensure that its conservation measures are implemented effectively, including the creation of Marine Conservation Zones.

We will be equally vigilant in ensuring the welfare of animals. We will promote the highest standards of farm animal welfare. We will work to reduce the use of animals in scientific research. We will promote responsible pet ownership by introducing effective codes of practice under the Animal Welfare Act, and target irresponsible owners of dangerous dogs.

To give wildlife greater protection, we will:

- firmly oppose any resumption of commercial whaling and do all we can to ensure that the international moratorium stays in place;

- press for a total ban on ivory sales and the destruction of existing stockpiles; and,

- promote new green spaces and wildlife corridors to help animals adapt and thrive in the face of climate change.

Protect habitats

The natural world faces great pressure from development and climate change. We will produce a White Paper on protecting the natural environment, including a focus on restoring habitat. We will pioneer a new system of conservation credits to protect habitats.

We will maintain national Green Belt protection, Areas of Outstanding Natural Beauty (AONBs), National Parks, Sites of Special Scientific Interest and other environmental designations which protect the character of our country's landscape. In addition, we will:

- review the governance arrangements for National Parks and AONBs to ensure that they are more accountable to local communities; and,

- work to reduce litter, which spoils too much of our countryside and urban environment.

Since 1997, the area of new woodland created in England each year has more than halved. In addition to ongoing woodland creation, we will launch a national tree planting campaign, planting up to one million new trees in the next Parliament. We will tackle illegal logging by:

- pressing for financial support from within a reformed EU budget to be given to developing countries to halt deforestation;

- pressing for only legally-harvested timber and timber products to be made available on the market; and,

- introducing a new criminal offence under UK law for the import and possession of illegal timber.

Promote sustainable and productive farming practices

Our farmland is a national resource for future generations and the foundation of our food security. We will prevent development on the most fertile farmland, in all but exceptional circumstances. To promote sustainable farming practices further, we will:

- support the Campaign for the Farmed Environment and seek to create a more effective system of environmental stewardship;

- ensure that consumers have the right to choose non-GM foods through clear labelling;

- not permit any commercial planting of GM crops until and unless it has been assessed as safe for people and the environment; and,

- develop a legally-binding protocol covering the separation of GM and non-GM material, including clear industry liability.

We will negotiate for further reform of the Common Agricultural Policy (CAP) to deliver greater value for money while supporting the sustainability of British farming. The new CAP should reflect the importance we attach to the environment, to ensuring food security and to tackling global poverty. We advocate the dismantling of market-distorting subsidies at a pace that allows time for British farmers and producers in developing countries to adapt. We will minimise and reform on-farm inspections, and abolish the Agricultural Wages Board.

The most pressing animal health problem in the UK today is bovine tuberculosis (bTB), which has led to the slaughter of over 250,000 cattle since 1997. As part of a package of measures, we will introduce a carefully-managed and science-led policy of badger control in areas with high and persistent levels of bTB.

Government should take the lead by procuring more sustainably. We will ensure that food procured by government departments, and eventually the whole public sector, meets British standards of production, wherever this can be achieved without increasing overall costs.

We will introduce honesty in food labelling, if necessary through legislation, so consumers can be confident about where their food comes from. This will ensure that meat labelled as 'British' is born and bred in Britain, and raised to our high welfare standards. And we will promote local food networks so that homes and businesses can obtain supplies of locally-produced food.

We will ensure a fair market for food suppliers – especially farmers – by reducing the burden of regulation. To ensure the grocery supply code of practice is applied fairly, we will introduce an independent supermarket ombudsman.

Use natural resources responsibly

We will introduce a Responsibility Deal on waste – a voluntary arrangement among producers to cut back on the production of waste and improve its disposal – as we move towards our goal of a zero-waste society.

Households need new incentives to go green, so we will reward people who do the right thing by encouraging councils to pay people to recycle, while scrapping Labour's plans for new bin taxes on families. To help this happen, we will put a floor under the standard rate of landfill tax until 2020 to encourage alternative forms of waste disposal.

With a rising population and growing strains on our water supply, industry and customers alike need new incentives to conserve water. We will reform the water industry, and bring in new measures to encourage businesses and households to value this precious resource more highly, and protect poorer households from excessive rises in water bills.

To cope with the increased risk of flooding associated with climate change, we will take forward the findings of the Pitt Review to improve our flood defences, prevent unnecessary building in areas of high flood risk, and ensure the country is better equipped when flooding does take place.

Manchester

Manchester was the epicentre of the industrial revolution, and the first industrialised city in the world. Today, the city is a national symbol of successful urban regeneration. Over the past three decades, Manchester has undergone extensive urban renewal, transforming the city's canals, mills and warehouses into vibrant new commercial, residential, and cultural spaces – including the creation of the Imperial War Museum North (*pictured*). As a result of this regeneration, Manchester is one of Britain's most dynamic cities, and has been voted amongst the best places in the country to locate a business.

Promote our national interest

A stronger Britain in a safer world

A Conservative government will defend our national security and support our brave Armed Forces in everything they do. We will promote our national interest with an active foreign policy. We will work constructively with the EU, but we will not hand over any more areas of power and we will never join the Euro. We will honour our aid commitments and make sure this money works for the poorest nations.

This country possesses great assets and advantages – a permanent seat on the UN Security Council, a leading role in NATO, a strong relationship with the United States, a major role in the affairs of the EU, and Armed Forces that are the envy of the world. We are a global trading nation and home to the world's pre-eminent language.

But, looking a decade or two ahead, powerful forces of economics and demography elsewhere in the world will make it harder for us to maintain our influence. All this in a world that is becoming more dangerous, where threats as diverse as state failure, international terrorism and new forms of warfare are being amplified by the impact of climate change and the spread of nuclear weapons technology. In a world of shifting economic power and increased threats, the UK stands to lose a great deal of its ability to shape world affairs unless we act to reverse our declining status.

We no longer inhabit a world in which foreign and defence issues can be separated from domestically-generated threats. Instead, we live in a world in which dangers, events and actions abroad are inter-dependent with threats to our security at home. We must meet the threats we face with a concerted response from the state. That response cannot just come from how we conduct our foreign affairs, or organise our defence and internal security – it must cut across energy, education, community cohesion, health, technology, international development and the environment too.

Helicopters per 1,000 troops, Helmand Province, 2009

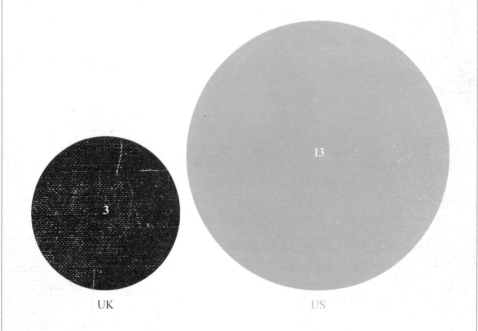

Source: The Times, Channel 4

Defend our security

We will create a National Security Council to oversee all aspects of our security, chaired by the Prime Minister. We are committed to succeeding in our mission in Afghanistan and will not leave our Forces without the resources they need to fulfil this goal. We will repair the Military Covenant with a series of measures to support service personnel, their families and veterans.

Labour have failed to deliver a unified and coherent approach to national security. They have not even kept their promise of a comprehensive National Security Budget. Their incompetence places our nation at risk. Despite fighting two major wars in the last decade, Labour have cut the target for the trained strength of the Army, shrunk the size of the Navy by a fifth and run down the RAF.

The men and women of our Armed Forces are the ones charged with protecting our nation's security. But Labour's dangerous mismanagement has endangered lives and harmed Britain's capacity to defend itself. Labour have been too slow to provide the equipment, such as helicopters, which our Forces on operations have badly needed. Our brave men and women, their families, and our veterans deserve the best for putting their lives on the line to protect our liberties. We will ensure they get the best.

A resilient nation

We understand the severity of the threats that exist and will do all we can to make Britain safe. We will establish a National Security Council to co-ordinate responses to the dangers we face, which will be chaired by the Prime Minister. In addition, we will:

- create a National Security Adviser and a new National Resilience Team for Homeland Security;

- develop a National Security Strategy and oversee a Strategic Defence and Security Review that implements that strategy; and,

- establish a new Permanent Military Command for Homeland Defence and Security to provide a more structured military contribution to homeland security.

Terrorism remains a major threat to our country and some of the biggest threats to our security do not come from abroad – they are home grown. A Conservative government will ban any organisations which advocate hate or the violent overthrow of our society, such as Hizb-ut-Tahrir, and close down organisations which attempt to fund terrorism from the UK. In Northern Ireland, we will continue to give our fullest support to the police and other agencies in their efforts to combat the threat from dissident republican and other terrorist organisations.

Support our brave Armed Forces

Our mission in Afghanistan is vital to our national security. Success in Afghanistan will be achieved when it is a more stable state, able to manage its own security, resist outside interference, and prevent terrorists from using its territory as a safe haven. We will always ensure our Forces have the resources they need to carry out their mission properly, and we will press other members of NATO to take their fair share of the military burden. The training of Afghanistan's own security forces is key to the success of the mission, and we will continue to make it a priority.

Our Strategic Defence and Security Review will ensure that resources for our Armed Forces are matched to our foreign policy requirements. We support the decision to renew Britain's submarine-based nuclear deterrent, based on the Trident missile system.

The hopeless mismanagement of defence procurement by this government has wasted billions of taxpayers' money and left our Armed Forces underequipped and dangerously exposed. We will review the structure of the Ministry of Defence to reduce running costs by 25 per cent. We will reform the procurement process to ensure the delivery of equipment on time and on budget. We will release spending on unnecessary and bureaucratic EU defence initiatives and spend the money on our Armed Forces. As part of that process, we will re-evaluate our position with the European Defence Agency.

Our commitment to look after the Armed Forces and their families – the Military Covenant – has been allowed to fall into disrepair. This is one of the most damning failures of Gordon Brown's government. We will restore the Military Covenant and ensure that our Armed Forces, their families and veterans are properly taken care of. To make that happen, we will:

- double the operational allowance;

- maximise rest and recuperation leave;

- ensure our servicemen and women are treated in dedicated military wards in hospital;

- change the rules so that service personnel are not locked out of the voting system by rules that Labour have introduced;

- use 'pupil level annual school census' data to include service children within our plans for a pupil premium in schools, ensuring they attract extra funding;

- provide university and further education scholarships for the children of servicemen and women killed while on active duty, backdated to 1990;

- pilot a mental health follow-up service for those who have left the services; and,

- review the rules governing the awarding of medals.

Iran

In Iran, hundreds of thousands of citizens calling for democratic reforms are using new technologies to come together, coordinate their protests against the state, and communicate with the outside world. The power of these information flows is growing rapidly. Every time the Iranian state has tried to choke the flow of information to dampen down the protests, people have turned to new technologies to share and access information. When the state cut off text messaging services, protesters switched to social media like Twitter and Facebook. When foreign journalists had their visas removed and had to leave the country, Iranians began to upload video clips onto YouTube so that the government's actions could continue to be scrutinised. And when the government tried to ban popular websites, private citizens outside Iran set up proxy internet servers so that Iranians could continue to access information.

A liberal Conservative foreign policy

We have great national assets and advantages to help us make the most of the opportunities we face and to deal with challenges. We will engage positively with the world to deepen alliances and build new partnerships. We will help reform international institutions, help those in need, and play our part in tackling climate change and the proliferation of military nuclear technology.

A Conservative government's approach to foreign affairs will be based on liberal Conservative principles. Liberal, because Britain must be open and engaged with the world, supporting human rights and championing the cause of democracy and the rule of law at every opportunity. But Conservative, because our policy must be hard-headed and practical, dealing with the world as it is and not as we wish it were.

Our approach to foreign affairs is based on a belief in freedom, human rights and democracy. We are sceptical about grand utopian schemes to remake the world. We will work patiently with the grain of other societies, but we will always support liberal values because they provide the foundations for stability and prosperity.

Protecting Britain's enlightened national interest requires global engagement. We will be safer if our values are strongly upheld and widely respected in the world. Our national identity is bound up in our historic global role as an outward-looking nation, giving generously to developing countries, and providing a safe haven to genuine refugees.

It is not in our character to have a foreign policy without a conscience or to turn our back on the millions who live in poverty and conflict.

Promote our enlightened national interest

A Conservative government will champion a distinctive British foreign policy. We will renew and reinforce our engagement with the rest of the world and build up British influence by deepening our alliances beyond Europe and the United States, not only diplomatically but in culture, education, commerce and security.

A Conservative government will always speak up for freedom and human rights. Torture is unacceptable and abhorrent, and we will never condone it.

We will support humanitarian intervention when it is practical and necessary, while working with other countries to prevent conflict arising.

Promoting Britain's interests and values means developing and strengthening our alliances and reforming international institutions. To achieve these goals, we will:

- work to establish a new special relationship with India, the world's largest democracy;

- seek closer engagement with China while standing firm on human rights;

- elevate our relationships with many friendly nations, including in the Middle East, as well as North Africa, South Asia and Latin America;

- press to keep the EU's doors open to those countries, including Turkey, that wish to join, conditional on the rigorous application of the accession criteria;

- support permanent seats on the United Nations Security Council for Japan, India, Germany, Brazil and African representation; and,

- strengthen the Commonwealth as a focus for promoting democratic values and development.

We will work with our allies across the world to prevent conflict and secure peace. We will maintain a strong, close and frank relationship with the United States. We will work closely with other European countries to establish a common approach to common problems, such as climate change. We will be committed to NATO as the ultimate guarantor of Europe's

security. To ensure our global security further, we will:

- work towards greater stability in Afghanistan and Pakistan;

- support concerted international efforts to prevent Iran from obtaining a nuclear weapon;

- support a two-state solution to the Middle East Peace Process;

- promote stability in the Western Balkans;

- always be ready to assist Cypriots in their efforts to agree a just, balanced and lasting settlement to reunite their island; and,

- play our part in efforts to make the world safer from the dangers of nuclear weapons and nuclear proliferation.

Total volume of UK trade

Trade with EU

Trade with the rest of the world

Source: Office for National Statistics, 2008

An open and democratic Europe

We will be positive members of the European Union but we are clear that there should be no further extension of the EU's power over the UK without the British people's consent. We will ensure that by law no future government can hand over areas of power to the EU or join the Euro without a referendum of the British people. We will work to bring back key powers over legal rights, criminal justice and social and employment legislation to the UK.

The European Union has done much to reconcile the painful division of Europe and to spread democracy and the rule of law across our continent. But it should not rest on those achievements.

European countries need to work together to boost global economic growth, fight global poverty, and combat global climate change. The European Union has a crucial part to play in enabling the countries of Europe to meet these great challenges of the 21st century. A Conservative government will play an active and energetic role in the European Union to advance these causes.

We will stand for open markets, and a strong transatlantic relationship; for an EU that looks out to the world, and that builds strong and open relations with rising powers like China and India. And, like every other Member State, we will fight our corner to promote our national interests.

We believe Britain's interests are best served by membership of a European Union that is an association of its Member States. We will never allow Britain to slide into a federal Europe. Labour's ratification of the Lisbon Treaty without the consent of the British people has been a betrayal of this country's democratic traditions. In government, we will put in place a number of measures to make sure this shameful episode can never happen again.

Restore democratic control

In future, the British people must have their say on any transfer of powers to the European Union. We will amend the 1972 European Communities Act so that any proposed future Treaty that transferred areas of power, or competences, would be subject to a referendum – a 'referendum lock'. A Conservative government would never take the UK into the Euro. Our amendment to the 1972 Act will prevent any future government from doing so without a referendum.

Unlike other European countries, the UK does not have a written constitution. We will introduce a United Kingdom Sovereignty Bill to make it clear that ultimate authority stays in this country, in our Parliament.

The Lisbon Treaty contains a number of so-called 'ratchet clauses', which allow the powers of the EU to expand in the future without a new Treaty. We do not believe that any of these 'ratchet clauses' should be used to hand over more powers from Britain to the EU. So a Conservative government will not agree to the UK's participation in the establishment of a European Public Prosecutor's Office or permit its jurisdiction over the UK. We will change the 1972 Act so that an Act of Parliament would be required before any 'ratchet clause' could be used. Additionally, the use of a major 'ratchet clause' which amounted to the transfer of an area of power to the EU would be subject to a referendum.

The steady and unaccountable intrusion of the European Union into almost every aspect of our lives has gone too far. A Conservative government will negotiate for three specific guarantees – on the Charter of Fundamental Rights, on criminal justice, and on social and employment legislation – with our European partners to return powers that we believe should reside with the UK, not the EU. We seek a mandate to negotiate the return of these powers from the EU to the UK.

Project Umubano

Every summer for the past three years, the Conservative Party has been running 'Project Umubano' in Rwanda. Over that period, Conservative MPs and volunteers have provided English lessons to 3,000 Rwandan primary school teachers, renovated a school, established a small medical library at Kirambi Health Centre, and built a community centre. Project Umubano is a sign of our commitment to One World Conservatism, and our belief in the positive power of social action.

Robert Halfon, pictured, is the Conservative candidate for Harlow

One World Conservatism

We will honour our commitment to spend 0.7 per cent of national income in aid, and ensure our aid is transparent and properly targeted. We will spend at least £500 million a year to tackle malaria. Both the British people and those who receive aid will get more control over how it is spent. We will push for a trade deal which brings growth to the poorest countries, helps those countries adapt to climate change, and puts in place the building blocks of wealth creation.

The global downturn has shaken up rich and poor countries alike. For poor countries, it threatens to undermine a decade's growth and poverty reduction. For rich countries, it puts new pressures on household and government budgets – nowhere more so than in the UK, where Labour's appalling mismanagement of the economy has saddled us with unprecedented levels of debt. But we should use this opportunity to reaffirm, not abandon, our values – which is why we will continue to increase the level of British aid. We will do so because it is in our national interest, as well as being the right thing to do.

Deliver on our commitment to the world's poorest nations

A new Conservative government will be fully committed to achieving, by 2013, the UN target of spending 0.7 per cent of national income as aid. We will stick to the rules laid down by the OECD about what spending counts as aid. We will legislate in the first session of a new Parliament to lock in this level of spending for every year from 2013.

We support the Millennium Development Goals and will continue to work towards them. We will maintain an independent Department for International Development (DFID) and keep aid untied from commercial interests. We will be completely transparent about the cost and performance of DFID programmes by independently evaluating programmes and by introducing, where appropriate, payment by results.

Our bargain with taxpayers is this: in return for contributing your hard-earned money to helping the world's poorest people, it is our duty to spend every penny of aid effectively. We will ensure British aid money is properly spent by publishing full details of British aid on the DFID website. This will include spending data on a project-by-project basis, published in an open and standardised format so that it can be used by third party websites. In addition, we will work to bring about improved transparency of aid spending by other development organisations.

We will create a new MyAid Fund to allow British people a direct say on aid spending, as well as giving people in developing countries more say over how aid is spent in their communities.

Under Labour, our aid funding is not used in a focused way, and is sometimes spent in countries that should be looking after their own poor citizens. So we will stop giving aid to China and Russia and review which other countries should get British aid. We will focus more on the poorest, paying particular attention to development within the Commonwealth.

A key aim of our aid is to make sure everyone gets access to the basics: clean water, sanitation, healthcare and education. We will focus particularly on the rights of women, children and disabled people to access these services. Malaria continues to kill nearly a million people per year, despite the fact that it is easily preventable and treatable. So, as part of our commitment to increase aid funding, a Conservative government will spend at least £500 million per year tackling malaria and will strongly support efforts to develop a malaria vaccine.

Trade and economic growth are the only sustainable way for developing countries to escape poverty, which is why we will put maximum effort into achieving an ambitious, pro-development global trade deal. Our aid programme will help poor countries put in

place the building blocks of wealth creation: property rights, effective public services, stability and the rule of law.

We will provide a more integrated approach to post-conflict reconstruction where the British military is involved – building on the Stabilisation Unit in Whitehall and creating a new Stabilisation and Reconstruction Force to bridge the gap between the military and the reconstruction effort.

To help deliver on our commitment to developing countries, we will:

- establish a Poverty Impact Fund to support innovative and effective British poverty-fighting groups which do not currently qualify for government funding;

- explore ways to help the very poorest developing countries take part in international climate change negotiations, and work to make our aid 'climate-smart';

- end Labour's use of the Export Credit Guarantee Department to support investment in dirty fossil fuel power stations, and instead use it to help spread new green energy technology to developing countries; and,

- encourage the establishment of a Pan-African Free Trade Area, which has the potential to transform that continent's economies.

ISBN 978-1-905116-05-8

9 781905 116058 >

ISBN No: 978-1-905116-05-8
© April 2010
Further copies may be obtained for £5.00 from Conservative Campaign Headquarters, 020 7222 9000.
Promoted by Alan Mabbutt on behalf of the Conservative Party, both of 30 Millbank, London SW1P 4DP.
Printed by Pureprint Group, Bellbrook Park, Uckfield, East Sussex TN22 1PL.